HOME COURT

OTHER TITLES BY BILL REYNOLDS

BIG HOOPS: A Season in the Big East Conference
(New American Library)

GLORY DAYS: On Sports, Men, and Dreams that Don't Die
(St. Martin's Press)

RISE OF A DYNASTY: The '57 Celtics, the First Banner,
and the Dawning of a New America
(New American Library, 2010)

HOPE: A School, a Team, a Dream
(St. Martin's Press)

BASKETBALL JUNKIE, a Memoir with Chris Herren
(St. Martin's Press)

STORY DAYS: Highlights from Four Decades Covering Sports
(Stillwater River Publications)

HOME COURT

The Best of Rhode Island Sports Through the Years

BILL REYNOLDS

Home Court: The Best of Rhode Island Sports Through the Years

Produced and printed by Stillwater River Publications.

Visit our website at **www.StillwaterPress.com** for more information.

First Stillwater River Publications Edition.

ISBN: 978-1-968548-43-8 (HARDCOVER)
ISBN: 978-1-968548-44-5 (PAPERBACK)

1 2 3 4 5 6 7 8 9 10
Written by Bill Reynolds.
Edited by Liz Abbott.
Cover photography by Ryan T. Conaty.
Cover & interior book design by Matthew St. Jean.
Published by Stillwater River Publications, West Warwick, RI, USA.

The views and opinions expressed in this book are solely those of the author and do not necessarily reflect the views and opinions of the publisher.

HOME COURT

"For over four decades at the Providence Journal, Bill Reynolds was a constant in Rhode Island life. He was the sports-page version of the Big Blue Bug. He was local and special and downright cool. He was Del's lemonade and coffee milk and any number of restaurants on Federal Hill. He could have gone to bigger, flashier places—look at the books he wrote, bestsellers, magic—but Providence was his set of comfortable clothes. He wore them with a familiarity, a grace, a grand curiosity that came through every word he wrote. All of this is obvious in *Story Days*. Check it out. It's like playing basketball with Ernie DiGregorio while Taylor Swift sings in the background. Fabulous!"

—LEIGH MONTVILLE, AUTHOR OF *TALL MEN, SHORT SHORTS*

"Bill Reynolds, a.k.a 'Shooter', is one of the great writers and basketball minds to grace the New England hoop landscape. The Boss told us Glory Days will pass you by. *Story Days* allows us to live it all again. Thanks, Shooter."

—DAN SHAUGHNESSEY, BOSTON GLOBE SPORTS COLUMNIST AND AUTHOR OF *WISH IT LASTED FOREVER*

OUR GAME: The Story of New England Basketball (Hall of Fame Press, 2006)

"Where some describe what they see or capture what they've learned, Reynolds is the rare scribe who did it himself and feels every bit of it. This is a basketball player with the gift of observation. The thrill of the race up-court or the last-second jumper comes back to anyone who ever played the game when they read *Our Game*."

—Doris Burke, ESPN basketball analyst

"Bill Reynolds is a man who has great feeling for the game of basketball. In *Our Game*, he dedicates himself to capturing all of the golden moments and characters of New England basketball. Trust me, Bill Reynolds is a winner!"

—Dick Vitale, ESPN/ABC TV commentator

STORY DAYS: Highlights from Four Decades Covering Sports (Stillwater River Publications, 2023)

"What set Bill Reynolds apart was his ability to descend on the biggest of the sports stages, peel away from the pack, explore the nooks and crannies of the event at hand, then emerge with the most poignant and eloquently written story of all. He is a New England literary treasure."

— Jackie MacMullen, author, former newspaper sports columnist and basketball analyst for ESPN.com

COUSY: His Life, Career and the Birth of Big-Time Basketball (Simon & Schuster, 2005)

"(an) insightful, well-written biography...Reynolds does a remarkable job illuminating the sport's early days in the 1940's... But the book's best parts are those in which Reynolds illuminates how Cousy's impoverished 1930's youth...created in him a drive to succeed..."

—Publishers' Weekly

"Voluble, basketball-savvy tour of Boston Celtic great Bob Cousy's life...Reynolds does a beautiful job of painting Cousy, right down to his French lisp...Not only an insightful biography, but a shining history of the early NBA as well."

—Kirkus Reviews

'78: The Boston Red Sox, a Historic Game, and a Divided City (New American Library, 2009)

"Reynolds does a superb job of stitching this baseball story into the larger tapestry of racial unrest that had Boston seething thirty years ago."

—Dayton Daily News

"(A) wide-ranging, zeitgeist-laden account of the terrible year that saw the Red Sox in first place in the American League East by a wide margin in July and humbled by the despised Yankees in October."

—The Boston Globe

PRAISE FOR BILL REYNOLDS' BOOKS

FALL RIVER DREAMS: A Team's Quest for Glory – A Town's Search for Its Soul (St. Martin's Press, 1994)

"Reynolds uncovers, in a moving and sensitive book, the desperate values of a city whose only dream is basketball glory."
—Newsday

"A marvelous book."
—The Boston Globe

"Poignant."
—USA Today

"Reynolds does a fine job...*Fall River Dreams* illustrates that sports can provide marvelous highs, but the joy of achievement can be supplanted by the desperate need to win — again and again and again."
—The New York Times

LOST SUMMER: The '67 Red Sox and the Impossible Dream (Warner Books, 1992)

"A treasure...written with such grace and humanity that it reads like a novel."
—Doris Kearns Goodwin, author of The Fitzgeralds and the Kennedys

"A terrific book."
—Leigh Montville, Sports Illustrated

CONTENTS

2000-2010

2010-2019

FOREWORD

POLLY REYNOLDS

I don't know who you are or where you live, but you'll not regret spending some time in the life of my brother Bill Reynolds in *Home Court*, a collection of his Rhode Island columns spanning forty years.

As his sister, I grew up to the beat of Billy's basketball on the driveway, the dependability of a Providence Journal newspaper on the kitchen table each morning, and the quirky stories of Rhode Island, some as familiar as a neighbor or a 'Gansett.

I loved and miss them all. I've heard since Billy's passing that many people feel the same. Welcome to the time warp of *Home Court*, where once again you can feel like you did back when Bill was writing his sports columns for the Journal.

Home Court is about going back in time, not forward and, in my opinion, that's a good thing.

The last half of the last century moved fast and outward and not much escaped its expanse. Soundtracks morphed from Perry Como to techno-pop; transportation evolved from Volkswagen Beetles to rent-a-rocket spaceships. People welcomed total reachability with their cell phones, trackers, and answering machines. They lost their privacy, too, but didn't seem to care, running towards the cameras about anything it seems. The world shrunk with technology. Everything spun weird and wild.

But not Bill Reynolds.

His jukebox was stuck on Roy Orbison, his slacks remained black, his shirts purple. There were always shorts and sneakers in his trunk, always a game in his future and baloney for lunch. Always old friends on the phone and always time for a memory.

Billy didn't like to fly or travel or chase mega events. To him domes were for desert dwellers and Superbowls for superfans only. His idea of an Open was a topless fancy sandwich. He was not dazzled by starshine. The peeps he wanted to see were the same ones he'd seen since grammar school. And every teammate from every team since.

The ego-less brother I knew was truly a naturally decent creature with a keen eye and a keener ear. He had an athletic gift he bent towards basketball, a love of language and a chameleon's intent to fit in. He made himself into a reliable outside shooter through endless dedication and repetitious effort, often in our Barrington driveway. He made himself into a writer the same way, working from the inside out.

Billy was always drawn to distinct and unusual stories which Rhode Island is full and proud of. He honored the old ways and old places, and wove them into something warm and recognizable, sometimes even colorful. He traveled the roads and the neighborhoods and kept track of the legends that populate our smallest landmass.

So this not just a sports book, though it's got a lot of great sports stories. Nor is it a travelogue, though it covers plenty of distance. It is time travel via stories written by a great storyteller. Born in the middle of major change and transience, the writer-dude, my brother, chose to stay home and pay attention. Like a firefly in an evening sky, Billy illuminated things most of us missed.

Some of the names in *Home Court* might be familiar to readers—Tommy Garrick, Davey Lopes, and Chris Herren, to name a few. But other might come as a surprise: Did you know Frank Caprio, the judge famous for his reality TV show about Providence's traffic court, always kept a photo of his Classical High wrestling team on his office wall? Or that the world's oldest Olympian lived in a Cranston suburb?

Or that Eddy Jamiel, known as "Fast Eddy," the trainer to the basketball players whose ankles he wrapped at Brown and Providence College, once played the national anthem on a trumpet at a Brown game?

Billy was a moth to such candles. Always curious, always looking and listening, scratching notes. Always up for the game.

He was an Everyman, ever attentive and empathetic. He felt the life-long bonds that teammates share because he had been there himself, from little league and basketball teams in Barrington to Brown University, where he was a co-captain for the Bears. He brought himself to his writing and this made him special. His stories also resonate because Billy knew his craft well enough to stay out of their way.

Reading *Home Court* brings me back to awe and admiration and respect for the lives good people live. My brother Billy led a charmed life and shared the secrets.

I am thankful to Liz Abbott for collating *Home Court*, a sequel to a first collection, *Story Days*. That book was well received because the truth is people miss Bill Reynolds, both the writer and the man.

I know I do.

EDITOR'S NOTE

LIZ ABBOTT

I'm almost embarrassed to say how this book came about. To honor Bill Reynolds, the late, great sports columnist for Providence Journal, I published a collection of his columns in 2023 called *Story Days*. In doing that book, I put aside columns that I thought were "too local," even creating a file called "Rejects," I'm ashamed to say. But I have since realized that those so-called rejects were pure gold, not only because of the grace and skill with which Bill always wrote about his subjects, but also because they provide an invaluable record of fascinating people and places in Rhode Island's sports history.

Who am I talking about? I'm talking about people like Johnny Britto, whose basketball talent brought him to the Harlem Globetrotters for a time, but who is equally remembered for his devotion to the kids in his Providence neighborhood of Fox Point.

I'm talking about the "Pere De Hockey," Father Adelard, whom Bill interviewed when he was 100 years old, and who is credited with introducing hockey to Rhode Island. Then there's Amby Smith, the longtime sports editor for of the Pawtuxet Valley News, who liked to call himself Chief Spucky Do. And John Coughlin, also known as the Phantom Friar, who graciously fought a cancer diagnosis away from the spotlight.

On and on it goes, an extraordinary array of local athletes and coaches, some of whom will be known to readers, others not, but that's the point. Bill found subjects whom he believed deserved to be noticed, their everyday courage or disappointments worthy to explore. This is Rhode Island sports history as only Bill could write it, with his humor, warmth and insight into the struggles people face as they try to achieve their dreams.

As many have noted since his passing in July, 2023, Bill could have gone to bigger newspapers and glitzier media platforms with his abundant talent. But he was a Rhode Islander through and through, cherishing the people that he encountered in his home state. Thanks to a boundless curiosity, he was endlessly interested in the people he met here, and felt it was an honor to tell their stories.

As a former Providence Journal reporter, I reserved the right to include stories Bill wrote about his co-workers over the years. These include columns on longtime copyeditor Emil John, sports columnist Bill Parillo and sports writer Ed Duckworth. I also included a few columns in which Bill reflects on the central role sports played in his own life. In these pieces, readers can glimpse a different side of Bill, one that is literary by nature, deeply reflective and an athlete at heart.

There will never be another Bill Reynolds in Rhode Island. Of this I'm sure. Changes in the newspaper industry make it unlikely that anyone can roam the sports range as freely as Bill did. But it's also improbable because Bill's outlook was so unique and, yes, so uniquely Rhode Island. Hence *Home Court*.

I hope you enjoy it.

1980-1989

A FRIENDSHIP THAT NEVER ENDS

1989

"Wherever I go for the rest of my life,
Dennis Lynch goes with me."
—Robert Williams

PROVIDENCE — I first met Robert Williams last December.

It was at a book signing in the Players' Corner Pub in downtown Providence, people waiting in line. One of them was a black kid whom I recognized from the North Providence summer league. He had played the last couple of summers for HKB Market, a team dominated by the Lynch brothers of Pawtucket, Billy, Patrick, John, and Dennis.

"What are you doing here?" I asked.

"I'm buying a Christmas present for my ex-coach."

"Who's that?"

"You know him," he said. "Dennis Lynch."

Last week Dennis Lynch died. He was 33 years old, and had been the basketball coach at St. Raphael Academy in Pawtucket for nine years. He also was one of those special people who touch more lives than they ever realize. His wake was a testimony to that, a cross-section of people whose lives, at some point, intersected with Dennis Lynch's.

But I couldn't stop thinking of Robert Williams, who had taken the time last December to come into downtown Providence and stand in line to buy a Christmas present for a man who used to be his high school coach.

So Sunday night I went up to the North Providence summer

league to see Williams. He is still playing on the same team with the Lynch brothers, HKB Market. Not that it's surprising that the Lynch brothers are again playing this summer. Dennis wouldn't have wanted it any other way. Last summer, after the cancer had been diagnosed, Dennis Lynch played in the league. This past season, as the cancer continued to weaken him, he still played basketball after almost every St. Ray's practice.

It was a hot night. HKB had lost, and Williams, his shirt stained with sweat, was getting ready to leave.

"How close were you with Dennis Lynch?"

He looked up, surprised.

"I loved Dennis," he said. "Dennis was like a brother to me. For the past two years I lived with him every day."

Williams met Lynch when he was about 12. His CYO team won the New England championship, and Dennis's father, then the mayor of Pawtucket, had arranged for a small ceremony.

"Dennis was there and we just hit it off," he said.

So began what on the surface seemed an unlikely friendship. The white son of the mayor, and a young black kid without a father from Prospect Heights, a dismal housing project where the future too often stopped at next week.

"After that he always sort of checked up on me," said Williams. "He'd jog up to Prospect Heights and find out what I was doing. Those couple of years I probably saw him once a week. I guess I was a little rough around the edges, being from the projects and all. Dennis sort of took care of me. He took me to play basketball with his brothers. He always stuck up for me."

In the eighth grade Williams passed a test to go to St. Ray's, and the next year he began going to school there. The friendship deepened. Williams also played football, and many nights after practice he would go over Lynch's house, have dinner, do his homework, take Lynch's car back to Prospect Heights, then pick up Lynch for school in the morning. Lynch took him to basketball games, basketball camp, everywhere. Williams worked on Billy Lynch's campaign to win election to the city council. Dennis Lynch would go places, and bring Robert Williams with him.

Lynch often talked to him about the importance of doing well in school, and working hard, and having discipline, and planning for the future, all those concepts that never seemed important back in Prospect Heights. Most of all, Lynch brought Williams into his life.

"I became like part of his family," Williams said. "Thanksgiving I would go over his mother's house for dinner and there would be a nameplate that said 'Robert' on it. His entire family accepted me."

His relationship with Lynch also gave him credibility. No longer was he just another kid from the projects. He was Dennis Lynch's friend.

"Dennis was the most giving person in the world," Williams said. "He is someone I could cry to."

When Williams graduated from St. Ray's, Lynch arranged for him to go to prep school, to St. Thomas More in nearby Connecticut. But Williams didn't like it. So, two weeks later Lynch helped him get into the Community College of Rhode Island. About that same time, he moved in with Lynch. During the days he went to CCRI. At nights he went back to live in Lynch's house.

Sometime last year Lynch discovered he had cancer. In a sense Williams went into denial. After all, wasn't Lynch still beating him one-on-one? Wasn't he still jogging and working out? Wasn't he still going about his life every day like his cancer was just another opponent you could beat if you had the right game plan?

"People would ask me how he was and I always said he was doing fine," he said. "I was never straight with anyone."

Throughout the school year, Williams starred on a great CCRI basketball team that went to the national tournament, a quick 5-foot-8 point guard. He also continued to live with Dennis, his wife, Laurie, and their infant son. One of the family. And Dennis

Lynch continued to teach him things. Only this time it was about courage.

"He taught me about being a person," Williams said softly. "About living every day like it's your last."

The past month or so, when the family knew Dennis was dying, the three brothers often would go afternoons to St. Ray's to play pickup basketball. In a sense the games became a sanctuary, a place away from the questions about Dennis. Williams went with them, one of the inner-circle. He was there when Dennis Lynch came home from the hospital, came home for the last time. He also was in the room when Dennis Lynch died. At the funeral he was a pallbearer.

Williams graduated from CCRI last Thursday.

"I just didn't go there," he said, the pride unmistakable in his voice. "I graduated."

He stopped, and his voice took on a far-away quality, like he was thinking of something else.

"I wish he had been there to see it."

In September, Williams will either go to Bryant or Southeastern Mass, off to college, far away from Prospect Heights. And in a sense Dennis Lynch goes to. For as Robert Williams says, "Wherever I go for the rest of my life, Dennis Lynch goes with me."

RISD NADS

1988

"Practice? Oh, we never practice."

—BILL CLIFTON

PROVIDENCE — My first clue that something a little different was going on here was the guy in the tan parka who began throwing pucks on the ice a minute before the game was going to start.

"Well, at least we got pucks," he said, as several players began skating on the smooth ice.

"Are you the coach?" I asked.

"I'm the pseudo coach," said Bill Clifton.

"The what?"

"I'm really not much of a coach," he said with a smile. "But then again these guys don't really want a coach either."

"So you don't practice a lot then?"

"Practice?" he said. "Oh, we never practice. There's no reason for them to practice."

Welcome to hockey at the Rhode Island School of Design, a club team that's been playing off and on for about 25 years now, about as far away from the spotlight as you can get. They are called the "Nads," and they are billed in the RISD student guide as the school's "infamous" hockey team.

And they are about as unique a college team as you will find anywhere.

There is no practice. Nor is there any mandatory attendance at the games, the unwritten rule being that if you have something more important to do, then do it, and come back next week. The schedule is kind of made up as the season goes along. Everyone who wants to play is invited.

Right from the time I first heard of them I had been intrigued with the idea of the Nads. After all, you think of RISD, the prestige art school complete with all the trappings, and a lot of images come to mind. Sports is not one of them. You think of RISD and you think of kids talking about abstract expressionism and angst, not power plays and blue lines. Kids who may want to be stars in a museum someday, but not in athletic contests.

So one night last week I asked Lisa Billard, a RISD senior, if she knew any information about the Nads. She called the apartment of two of the players, and came back shaking her head.

"So?" I said.

"Sorry," she said. "They weren't available. One of them is pre-disposed, and the other is out in the back yard setting a squirrel trap."

Oh.

On this Sunday night at Meehan Auditorium at Brown, minutes before they are to play Johnson and Wales, there are 23 Nads all dressed up in maroon uniforms they bought themselves. There also are about 50 students in the stands.

"How many of your kids take this seriously?" I asked Clifton.

"Maybe five," he said. "But they all play their hearts out. Some are not in the greatest condition, but they all try."

Clifton, whose wife is assistant director of housing at RISD, grew up around hockey in Wisconsin. When he heard the Nads were looking for a "pseudo-coach" he signed up. Now he was trying to figure out how many players he's going to have tonight.

"Probably not that many," he said. "We're in exams. Kids have a lot of things to do."

You can call the Nads' roster eclectic. It includes everyone from a few kids who played in high school, to kids who only played street hockey, to kids who never skated before, to two alumni in their 40's, one of whom started the Nads in 1964. His name is Ray Sauer, he is 47, and in real life he teaches at New England Tech. He played high school hockey in Warwick back in the '50s, and essentially has been playing ever since, going by the old adage that once hockey gets in your blood it's there forever. Last year he was studying one night in the RISD library, saw a sign for the Nads, and here he is.

Not that he's the only great story on the Nads.

Another is Ken Bruce, class of '71.

He is 43, and never skated until a couple of years ago. But he always was one of those guys who talked about how much he wanted to play, to the point where his wife ultimately said, either shut up about it or do something about it. So here he is, loving it.

"I waited 20 years to play on a team," he said.

The Johnson and Wales players all wear different colored jerseys, and they score in the first minute. But the Nads come right back and tie it a few minutes later. If the players vary in ability, the game is spirited, intense, full of checks against the boards, and bodies flying across the ice.

The 50 or so students also are spirited. They yell at the Johnson and Wales players, they cheer when the Nads make a good play. If everything else about the Nads is as laid-back as a Californian on 'ludes, once the game starts everything changes. So after Carey Paik scores his third goal of the night and the Nads win, there is cheering and jubilation. Winning is fun, even at RISD.

Afterwards, Paik tells how he played in high school.

"So what keeps you playing?" I asked.

"It gets me out of the studio, and gets my mind on something else," he said.

"It's a blast," says Nick DeLuca, who never skated until he joined the Nads. "It's the best of both worlds. We are real serious when we play the games, but don't have to do any of the other stuff that comes with playing a sport in college."

Hockey, RISD style.

"By the way?" I asked Lisa Billard. "How come they're called the Nads?"

She gave me one of those looks you reserve for people who don't have a clue.

"So people can yell 'Go' at them," she said.

What did you expect from RISD, cheerleaders and sis-boom-bah?

JAMIE BENTON IS READY TO SOAR

1984

"He's one of the best we've seen,
and we've seen a lot of them."
—BC COACH GARY WILLIAMS

PROVIDENCE — The two little kids knew.

They were about eight and they were inside the gym at the Providence Boys and Girls Club last Thursday in South Providence watching a rugged kid about 19 shoot around.

"He's going to play for Boston College," said one of them.

"When?" the kid was asked.

"Next year," said the other. "That's Jamie Benton and he's going to play for Boston College next year."

Jamie Benton, twice an All-Stater at La Salle and now at Maine Central Institute, a prep school in Pittsfield, Maine, has quietly come from out of nowhere and become one of the best high school basketball players in the East.

As Boston College coach Gary Williams says, "He's one of the best we've seen, and we've seen a lot of them."

The irony is that not too many people around here are aware of it. The principal reason is that Benton, though twice an All-Stater at La Salle, essentially was a 5-foot-11 forward, a burly kid who seemed more suited to be a linebacker. Another example of a Rhode Island high school basketball player playing out of position in the state's schoolboy tradition of 6-4 centers and 5-11 forwards.

"We liked him as an athlete," remembers Rhode Island coach Claude English, "but he didn't handle the ball."

So Benton probably would have been overlooked the way Rhode Island kids Ernie DeWitt and Bobby Reitz were overlooked when they were coming out of high school several years back. Kids deemed either too small, two slow, two something. Except of one thing. Benton was also playing for an Amateur Athletic Union team from New Bedfored called Buddy's, playing in several AAU tournaments in Boston that are showplaces for college scouts. And unlike at La Salle, he handled the ball for the AAU team.

The game that changed his future came against Riverside Church, a New York City team comprised of high school All-Americans Henry Dalrymple and Kenny Smith, who now starts for North Carolina as a freshman. Not that Benton knew who they were. It was just another team, another game. Going head-on-head against Smith, he had 33.

"That's where we first saw him," remembers Williams. "He was a ballhandling guard and we were very high on him."

The he came back for his last season at La Salle, half of which he missed because he was scholastically ineligible. The other half again spent without handling the ball. When school ended last June he was a junior who had used up his high school eligibility. An athletic version of a man without a country, seemingly just another kid with potential and no grades whose career was going to be over at 18.

But Boston College assistant Kevin Mackey helped arrange for him to go to Maine Central, where former BC players Dwan Chandler and James Jackson had spent a year raising moribund grades. As late as last spring no one was involved with Jamie Benton except BC.

He was still the Great Unknown.

The Providence Boys and Girls Club is a red-brick building, known in the neighborhood as the Southside Boys Club. It's one of the meccas of basketball in South Providence, one of the places where kids first make their local reps long before they go on to play in high school. It has an alumni list that includes Dobie Dennis, Willie

Washington, Michael Hazard, Billy Perry, Rickyy Santos. Even Marvin Barnes. Guys who come out of tough, Darwinian worlds to cast a heavy imprint on high school basketball in the state.

"They all came through here at one time or another," says director Roosevelt Benton, Jamie's uncle, who once played for Central back in the mid-sixties.

And since Jamie's father had died when he was about three, and he lived within sight of the boys' club, Roosevelt became almost a surrogate father. The club also became a second home. Jamie played in all the kids' leagues, played with older kids, grew up chasing the inner-city basketball dream just like Dennis, Washington and Hazard had done before him.

"James was real chunky then, real wide," remembers Roosevelt Benton. "...when he played with older kids, he always played outside."

He still is chunky, about 5-11, 186, a John Bagley clone. That was evident this summer when Benton played in the state's premier outdoor league in North Providence. It also served as Venton's coming -out party, a basketball version of a debutante ball. Not only did he average over 20 points, he also ran his team, made clutch shots, did everything a quality guard's supposed to do. You didn't need to be Red Auerbach to know that Benton was not just Rhode Island high school good. He was really good.

"It's common knowledge among the street athletes that the local schools really aren't too interested in the local kids," says Roosevelt Benton. "But guys who have played with James were aware of his abilities. Older guys like Dennis who have taken him places to play. But I don't think too many other people were."

They are now. Now Benton has become the most highly recruited basketball player in the state since Joey Hassett in the early seventies. The week before he left, URI got involved. Now there is Marquette, Pittsburg, Northeastern, Maine. Providence College is not recruiting him because they have a slew of underclass guards and already have signed another, Matt Palazzi.

"We know he's a very good player, and he may turn out to be better than anyone we've got," says coach Joe Mullaney. "But guards are just not our greatest need right now."

Interestingly, Benton is getting this attention without having gone to any of the publicized showcase summer camps throughout the country, without the publicity machine players of similar ability get.

"It's starting to accelerate now," says Roosevelt Benton. "Now they're starting to jump off the phone at him. And they're also starting to talk about playing time."

Maine Central even played a game against Boston College against the jayvees before Christmas. Benton scored 23. Adding to the connection is that Maine Central has the same uniforms as BC, runs the same offense, used the same defense. Miniature Eagles. He's scheduled to visit BC January 14 and said the coaches already have told him that he is their second guard choice for next year.

"We want him to come in and back up Michael Adams next year, then start as a sophomore," says BC coach Williams.

Not that this is an easy year for Benton. Maine Central is in Pittsfield, in the middle of nowhere, a long way from South Providence. There isn't much to do and not many people to do it with. But he says he is doing well in school and Williams backs him up.

"He's not a bad student. He gets good grades," says Williams.

"The first month I wanted to come home, but I know this is what I have to do to get to Division 1," Benton says.

That's the important thing, he says. Because every weekend you can see Washington, Dennis and Perry playing at the Southside Boys Club. Players with worlds of ability who, for one reason or another, never made it to Division 1.

"I can't remember anyone who went to Division 1," he says.

But that's were Jamie Benton is headed.

Just ask the two little kids.

TOMMY GARRICK: COMEBACK KID

1988

"I knew I had doubters, but I didn't care what other people thought."

—Tommy Garrick

WEST WARWICK — It seems an unlikely place to come looking for a basketball star.

But it is here, just a jump shot away from two of the stone mills along the Pawtuxet River that once defined this old mill town, that Tom Garrick grew up.

Tommy Garrick, the only Rhode Islander on the University of Rhode Island basketball team, is the best player to come out of Rhode Island in the past decade.

And if this is an unlikely place, then maybe that is only fitting. For this is an unlikely story. It includes a 68-year-old blind man who never has seen his wife of 42 years, or any of his eight children, but still goes to all his son's games. It includes the first black family to live in West Warwick, pioneers in this community long noted for its rigid ethnicity. It includes a family that has stayed together, through the good times and the bad.

It also includes, as the best stories often do, a redemption story. It is a basketball redemption story about the local kid who goes off to the state university, his head full of high school cheers, only to struggle his first two years. Struggle to the point that maybe he would have quit, if not for this family that has shaped him, defined him, then guided him through the bad times. Because that is Tommy Garrick, too.

In a sense, Garrick has become the most obvious symbol of the resurgence of the URI basketball program. The hometown kid helping to lead a basketball program out of the wilderness. Is there a connection between URI's current basketball fortunes and the emergence of Tommy Garrick as one of the better college players in the East? Maybe. For this is all about having to prove it, and fighting for respect, and finally starting to get recognition.

The story begins long before Tommy Garrick ever shot a basketball. Maybe it begins in 1943, when the older Thomas Garrick, who had grown up in South Carolina, lost his sight in a land-mine explosion outside of Berlin in World War II. He was sent to a hospital in Valley Forge, Pa. There, he met his wife, Beatrice. She was the hostess at the hospital, had grown up in Philadelphia.

In 1955, the Garricks moved to Rhode Island, where Thomas had gotten a job at Quonset repairing radar machines. They began raising a family. Simple, but not as easy as all that. They had trouble getting an apartment in Providence. Later, they had trouble buying a house in Warwick.

"People saw we were colored," Thomas Garrick says simply.

He and Beatrice are sitting in this blue house on West Warwick's Providence Street, just down from the Bradford Soap Works. Nearby are the row houses where fingers of time have sullied the paint. The living room is dominated by family pictures. They compete for attention with Tommy's trophies. The Garricks moved here in 1966, six months before Tommy was born.

West Warwick is a town that sprouted along the banks of the Pawtuxet River. Every time the river turned, there was a new mill, complete with a new ethnic group to work in it. The new workers, in turn, began their new communities, different villages with their own identities, each autonomous. Maybe not the easiest town for the first black family.

For a long time, there was a neighbor who never said a word to them. Another never said a word to the day he died. Year after year of never saying a word. And in the beginning, the five oldest Garrick children constantly wondered why they were in this small town where they were the only blacks.

"I used to tell them not to worry about that," says Beatrice Garrick. "That they were here to learn."

The oldest child was named Sonny. He was already in high school when Tommy was born, played basketball for West Warwick High School.

"Sonny was the pioneer," says Beatrice Garrick. "He paved the way for the others."

Tommy is the youngest, the only other boy. He and his sister Stacey were the only black kids in the Horgan Elementary School.

"I never really thought about the fact there were no black kids until high school because I grew up with it," Tommy Garrick says. "There were a couple of racial incidents in elementary school, but the principal and vice principal never let it get out of hand. I think it was because everyone knew my family, knew we were a good family.

"Everyone in West Warwick knew the Garricks," Tommy continues. "I was happy where I was. We were just normal kids in the neighborhood. And every Sunday we went to church in Providence and spent a lot of time with blacks, so I always thought I had the best of both worlds. I have very fond feelings of West Warwick. It is my home."

He was never a street kid. His life revolved around family, going to the Ebenezer Baptist Church on Sundays, doing well in school, working hard, and being a good person.

Maybe it was because, being black in West Warwick, the Garricks knew they always had to be a little better than the family down the street. Maybe it was because, in a sense, they always needed one another. Maybe it was because the head of the household was blind, which meant everyone had to help out. But there's always been a special closeness.

"I think I was 10 or 11 before I really realized what my father being blind meant," says Garrick. "I guess up until then, I took it for granted. I mean, he couldn't go play catch with me, but my father has always been there for me. I've never felt I've missed anything because he was blind."

In junior high, Doug Haynes, the former URI football player, and his brother moved to West Warwick. Now there were four black kids in the school. In high school, there were five black kids, four on the basketball team. One of them was Garrick's nephew, Paul Gonsalves, Sonny's son. Garrick began playing basketball in the fifth grade, introduced by his older brother, Sonny.

He also grew up with the Providence College Friars. It was the mid- '70s, the time of Joey Hassett and Bruce Campbell, sellout crowds in the Providence Civic Center. If URI basketball also was doing well at the time - it was an era that featured Sly Williams - it was the Friars who were on television. It was the Friars the kids tried to emulate on the playgrounds. And Tommy Garrick was no different; he dreamed of playing for the Friars.

Garrick was the only sophomore starter on the West Warwick High School team. But he didn't want his family to come see him play because he didn't want to embarrass them - he didn't think he was playing well enough. The next year, he was All-State. As a senior, he was the best player in Rhode Island, teaming up with his nephew and Haynes to lead West Warwick to the state Class B title. But the knock on him was he was a 6-foot-3 forward in a weak league, someone who was a great high school player because he was more physical than the kids he was playing against, more athletic. Certainly, that's what Providence College thought.

The Friars were struggling in the Big East Conference at the time, desperately seeking high school players with impressive resumes, not some kid from West Warwick. In the winter of 1984, Steve Hocker, then a PC assistant coach, went to see Garrick play.

"One night we were playing East Greenwich and I looked in

the stands and saw coach Hocker there," Garrick says, "and I knew what he was there for. At least I thought I knew what he was there for. I thought I played well that night. Scored 28 or 30 points. Had my first two-handed dunk in a game. But I never heard anything."

He wondered what he had to do to get recruited. But if PC didn't want, him he would go someplace that did. But where?

He was a Rhode Island kid from a suburban league that rarely sends anyone off to college basketball, never mind Division I. He was headed for Bryant, a Division II team where his brother had played. But Brendan Malone, who had just been hired as the new URI coach, saw Garrick play in an AAU tournament, liked the fact "he played with intensity," and figured it might be good public relations for URI to give a scholarship to the best high school player in Rhode Island. Even if no one was really too sure about his future.

"I knew I got in the back door at URI," says Garrick, "but I felt I could play Division I basketball. I had grown up watching Division I games on TV and I wanted to be on TV and in the news. I knew I had doubters, but I didn't care what other people thought."

The next fall, Tommy Garrick took his game to Kingston, the only Rhode Islander on the URI team. He also came into a basketball program that was all but on life support. There had been three losing seasons in a row, the last one, 6-22. Claude English had just been fired as the coach. Malone, a former assistant at Syracuse, had been hired to pump some life back into the program. The Rams had become a bad team that played in the Atlantic 10, a low-profile league in the shadow of the glamorous Big East Conference. Out of sight, out of mind. Off the charts nationally, overshadowed in its own state by Providence College.

Arriving with Garrick was Carlton Owens, a street-smooth point guard from Coney Island who still carried a bullet in his left arm, a legacy from a neighborhood that had become the underbelly of the American dream. He was Malone's first recruiting gem. Owens quickly became the best player on the team, a preview of the future. Garrick played sporadically his first year. He seemed tentative, unsure. He was now forced to play guard, a new position for him. In a sense, he was a victim of being the best player in Rhode Island, his game lacking the polish it would have gotten in a more competitive area. Often, he was just another player off the bench.

"I had to put my pride behind me," he says. "To swallow it."

In his first two years, the Rams were 17-39, and Garrick was just another player on a mediocre team. He always worked hard, he always hustled, but maybe all the doubters had been right. He even flirted with playing football instead, a sport he had played one year in high school, making All-State.

"I was depressed," he says. "I was starting to doubt my ability. But what got me through was I always knew my family was behind me whatever happened. That they didn't care whether I had basketball or not."

Last year changed everything. Owens continued to be Owens. Kenny Green, a Connecticut kid who had been red-shirted the year before, became one of the best inside players in the East. Bonzie Colson, 6-9, from suburban Washington, D.C., added a presence inside. John Evans, 6-5, from Cambridge, Mass., added some quickness inside. Tom Penders replaced Malone, who went off to be an assistant coach with the New York Knicks, and immediately changed the style of play, creating a faster, more-up-tempo team. But the key was the development of Garrick.

By the end of the year, the Rams had won 20 games for the first time since 1981, and Garrick had become one of the top players in the East. All of a sudden, he was doing to college teams what once he had done to East Greenwich and Cranston West. The hometown kid was resurrecting the hometown team. But as fate would have it, all this was taking place in a season when PC was going to the Final Four, as if URI was destined always to be overshadowed by PC, no matter what they did.

Now, it's the other way around. The Rams are 17-2, having one of their best seasons, and already in the top 20 teams in the country in a couple of polls. They have crushed Providence College, establishing their in-state dominance for the first time in many a year. And they finally seem to be getting the respect they have sought for so long. And Garrick is living in the middle of a basketball fantasy, one that's belonged to only a select handful.

Ernie DiGregorio.

Marvin Barnes.

Joey Hassett.

The list of locals who have made a significant imprint on big-time college basketball is a small one. Garrick is now on that list.

"Things couldn't have worked out any better for me," he says. "Who knows what might have happened if I had gone somewhere else?"

But it is even more than that. His family is living his success, too. Not only do they know they helped Tommy through a difficult time, a time when his team was losing and his career seemed in limbo, they have been a part of it. They have seen him evolve from a tentative college freshman to a poised and successful team leader. They've seen him become everything Thomas and Beatrice Garrick wanted their children to be when they moved to West Warwick so many years ago. Now they come to every game. Someone always sits with Thomas Garrick, broadcasts the game to him, just as someone in the family has done since Tommy was in junior high school.

For he is 68 now, Thomas Garrick is, and has, in the words of his wife, "been close to death several times." But now, he hears the cheers for his youngest child and says he "feels blessed."

PAPPY OWENS GETS HIS DEGREE

1988

"I used to call them basketball bums, and I didn't want to be a basketball bum."

—Pappy Owens

KINGSTON, R.I. — He thinks he made up his mind one night before Christmas a year ago. He was home in Philadelphia at the time, working a night shift for UPS, loading mail trucks in a place they call the Hub. It's a place where a supervisor walks overhead on a catwalk, with floodlights everywhere, and, in his words, "looks like a (prisoners) camp."

It was there that Horace "Pappy" Owens told himself that maybe it was time to go back to school and get his degree. Time to go back to Kingston, back to the place he had left four years earlier as one of the greatest basketball players in the history of the University of Rhode Island. Back when he was a second-round draft choice of the New Jersey Nets and he looked into the future and saw professional basketball, not loading UPS mail trucks in the Hub.

So last fall he came back to URI to finish school. He moved into a dorm room on campus, along with kids who didn't know who he was. He started going to class, trying to be a regular student in this place where he never had been a regular student. He was about to be 26 years old and the cheers were yesterday's memories.

"The first day I got here I asked myself, 'What am I doing here?' " he says. "I had good memories of URI and really felt I learned a lot here about all kinds of things. But I felt so out of place."

Everything looked the same. The campus. Keaney Gym. Everything. But it was not the same.

His future had seemed clearer when he left in the spring of '83 to go off to the Nets. But things quickly got complicated and started to turn sour. The Nets were in turmoil, looking for quick fixes, not rookies who needed nurturing. A few days before the season started, Owens was traded to the 76ers. He found out while watching television. Then, when he got to the Sixers, he quickly was informed there was no room for him, that the roster already was loaded with guaranteed contracts.

"It was a horror show," he says. "I was very, very angry. It was a rude awakening to the real world because I thought I never really had a chance. It wasn't that I had to go to work - I had gone to work every summer of my life - but I felt someone had taken something from me."

He went to work for the recreation department in Philadelphia. Then he was an assistant manager in a shoe store. For he did not want to go to the CBA, did not want to be the kind of guy who drifts from league to league, still chasing the game.

"I used to call them basketball bums," he says, "and I didn't want to be a basketball bum."

Every summer he lit up the Baker League in Philadelphia, letting everyone know he could still play. But that was it. There would be no CBA. No going to an NBA camp as a free agent, little more than fodder. No playing in Europe, drifting from league to league. No chasing rainbows.

In a sense, he was in a kind of shock. Basketball always had been everything to him. It kept him away from the gangs in his North Philadelphia neighborhood when he was a kid. It gave him an identity as an adolescent when he was one of the best young players in the city, a third-team, high-school All-American. It got him to college. Basketball always defined his life, and now he was watching it slide away, a little more with each passing season.

Periodically, he would give a thought to finishing his degree. For he didn't want to live out the stereotype of the ghetto kid who goes off to play big-time ball and returns four years later with a lot of memories and no degree. Just another do-you-remember story. His parents, who had always stressed education even when he saw only a basketball hoop in his future, suggested he go back to school. Temple coach John Chaney told him the same thing. Bob Terino, a URI alumnus instrumental in the recruiting of Owens, kept asking him when he was coming back to Rhode Island.

Then, last fall, Pappy Owens went back. URI honored the fifth year of his scholarship and Owens returned to school, 4 1/2 years after he had left for the NBA. And if he had the feeling this was "not my place anymore," he also had to face, for the first time since the fifth grade, going to school without being able to play basketball.

"The campus was humming the way it used to be," he says, "but it wasn't with my name anymore."

But he swallowed his pride, told himself he was there for a reason. And gradually he began to feel comfortable. He played pickup games with the players in the fall, was immediately accepted. Tom Penders welcomed him, made him feel a part of this year's team, the link to the glory days of the past. His professors have been wonderful, understanding. Everyone has been great. He no longer feels out of place.

So every day Pappy Owens gets up at 6:30, works out, goes to the dining hall, studies for a while and goes to class. Most afternoons he drives to Providence where he works part-time as a case worker in the Key Program, a Federal Hill program for disadvantaged kids. There he's known as Horace, not Pappy. There he's just another part-time case worker, not one of the greatest basketball players in URI history.

"I don't make a big deal out of it," he says.

He will graduate in June from URI with a degree in communications, probably will go back to Philadelphia where he already has a job in a social service agency. And, in a sense, the degree will mean more than if he had gotten it in 1983. Because he knows that now he has sacrificed for it. Has uprooted his life for it. Has come back to his past to find his future.

"I think coming back has been one of the best things that ever happened to me," says Pappy Owens.

"Maybe I wasn't meant to be a professional basketball player and it just took me a while to accept it. Sure, basketball is still important. It's just not my first priority anymore. I guess I just realize now that there are more important things."

FAST EDDIE TAPES TO A HAPPY TUNE

1988

"They all need a pat on the back."

—Eddie Jamiel

PROVIDENCE — The first time I met Eddie Jamiel was in some lost year in the mid-60's. I was playing basketball for Brown then, Eddie was the new trainer, and right from the beginning he was different.

There were rumors he was the son of a Lebanese sheik; rumors he once had been a professional prize fighter; rumors he was the black sheep of a family whose imprint was all over the town of Warren, Rhode Island; rumors he once had been a masseur in Miami.

We didn't know the specifics then, just that Jamiel was doing the work of five people, keeping everyone upbeat, even on a team when losing seemed to sleep under the bench. Eddie was a case study in joie de vivre, doing a hundred-and-one little things, the glue keeping it all together.

He also was one of those people you remember long after you forget most of the rest. Sports writers occasionally would come to talk to us players, but even back then I knew the best story on the team was Eddie. Oh yes. And we knew that no one ever taped an ankle quicker than this new trainer.

Fast Eddie.

So it seems a little strange to go to a Providence College practice - not a Brown practice - and not only see Jamiel out there on the floor, but also realize he has become the one constant of the Friars basketball team. The players come and the players go. The assistant coaches come and go. Joe Mullaney turned into Rick Pitino who turned into Gordie Chiesa who turned into Rick Barnes. Everything changes. And still there is Jamiel.

The man who tapes an ankle faster than anyone.

This affinity for hard work is a lesson he learned early. He grew up in Warren, the 10th of 13 children. His father and mother had come here from Lebanon when they were 15 and 14 years old, respectively, already married. His father also had been the mayor of a small town in Lebanon, a real live sheik. But when he came to this country, he worked at the old Converse rubber plant in Bristol. Seems there was not a great demand for sheiks. Soon he was selling shoelaces door-to-door, the beginning of an entrepreneurial spirit that has marked the family to this day.

Eventually, his father ran a clothing store in Warren. The family lived upstairs. Eddie slept in a bunkbed with two other brothers. When he was 13, he got some boxing gloves for Christmas. He put some rags in an old duffel bag, hung boxing pictures on the wall, read boxing books and started chasing a dream. His brothers dreamed of being lawyers and businessmen. He dreamed of being the champion of the world, the oldest sports dream of all.

"I was like the black sheep in the family," he says. "My family always were trying to talk me out of fighting."

He turned pro in 1957, after getting out of the Marines. He was 21 years old.

He was "Satch" Jamiel then, and he was different. He stuck his tongue out at his opponents. He stuck his chin out, dropped his hands, taunted. He did the Ali-shuffle long before anyone ever heard of Ali. He did the rope-a-dope. It was all part of his strategy to upset his opponent, get him out of his rhythm, then counter-punch.

"He was the best showman I ever saw," says sports writer Bill

Parrillo, who used to watch Jamiel fight on the undercards at the old Arcadia in downtown Providence.

The big names in Rhode Island boxing at the time were Willie Greene, George Araujo, Chubby Gomes. Jamiel sparred with all of them. He also eventually won the Rhode Island light-heavyweight crown. But professional boxing was life on a shoestring, a carousel of training, postponed fights, then training some more. Plus, all those endless hours of getting hit in practice, all those body blows the public never sees, all the punches that begin beating down the spirit. So when he had to fight some guy from Chicago one night at the last minute, after he had prepared for someone else, he went down in one round and didn't want to get up.

Requiem for a heavyweight.

In fact, his last fight was a three-rounder at Brown's Marvel Gym about a decade ago. Marvin Hagler, of all people, was the main event. Jamiel fought a Brown student, complete with being carried in on a chair. No one ever said Fast Eddie doesn't do things with a certain style. Once he played the National Anthem on the trumpet before a Brown basketball game. He had come to Brown as a trainer in 1965, after being a masseur in Miami. I met him shortly afterwards. He was trying to get better at his trade then, reading books on athletic injuries, studying, learning.

"Bring me a new word every day," he said to me then.

The first one I brought him was "euphemism."

"What's it mean?" he asked.

"It's a different way of saying something," I said. "Like saying 'pass away' when you really mean 'die.' "

The vocabulary lessons soon stopped. But to this day virtually every time I see him he yells "euphemism" at me.

Jamiel came over to PC with Joe Mullaney in 1982. Maybe there had been too many late-night bus rides and eating box lunches in the back of buses in the middle of nowhere. Meals of stale ham-and-cheese sandwiches, brownies a week old, and one Coke, not two. All the things that comprised basketball at Brown back then. Or maybe it was just time for a change.

"I loved the Brown kids and at first I thought the PC kids would be different," he says. "But I quickly realized that an 18-year-old kid is an 18-year-old. They all want to do well. They all cry when they are hurt. They all need a pat on the back. There's no difference."

So now he's in his seventh year with the Friars, a steady presence through the incredible roller-coaster that has been Providence College basketball the last six years.

"I shake hands when they arrive and I shake hands when they leave," he says with a rueful smile. "I've seen it all. The training meals. The travel. The post-game chalk-throwing, orange-slinging tirades. All of it. But my main job never has changed. And that is to keep the head coach happy. Because that's the secret. Try and keep everyone happy and make it easy for the coach."

And through it all he survives, still as upbeat and unique as he was when I first met him 20 years ago. Back when he was the new trainer at Brown and could tape an ankle faster than anyone.

HOW CAN YOU NOT TAKE THE PATS WITH NINE?

1986

"The whole nation's going to bet this game. From the wise guys in Vegas to old ladies in nursing homes ..."

—Anthony the Handicapper

SOMEWHERE IN RHODE ISLAND – "Have I bet the Pats?" asks Anthony the Handicapper. "It's like they've been giving it away. Like picking plums off a tree."

"So you playing them again?" asks the guy in the red shirt.

"How can you not? How can you not take them with 9 1/2 points?"

"Yeah, but the Bears are the Bears, know what I mean?" says red shirt. "A lot of the services like the Bears."

"Services?" says Anthony the Handicapper, his voice rising in exasperation. "They should all be in jail. They get some legitimate worker to believe that garbage. Anybody who talks about a lock should be locked up and put in an institution. For robbing the public."

Anthony the Handicapper shakes his head, wondering at the puzzlement of it all.

"Go against the Pats?" he continues, incredulity running through his voice. "How can you do that? I've become their biggest fan."

Not really.

Anthony the Handicapper is not a fan. No way. Leave the cheering and the slogans for the suckers. He is a handicapper, an evaluator of games. Sure, it's nice that the home team is in the Super Bowl. That's nice. Just like cute puppy dogs and pretty ribbons are nice. What's important is that they've beaten the point spread 14 weeks in a row.

And, sure, he also puts money down on games, but don't tell him he's a gambler. Gamblers are action junkies, guys who want to bet West Coast games so they can have action while they sleep. Anthony the Handicapper is a professional.

"A professional looks for a spot, an edge," he says. "A degenerate bets like he has four hands. They call you and say 'Any action on this?' They're always saying "What else you got? What else? That's their middle name. What else?' They're maniacal bettors. One guy calls me up and wants to know if he can bet rugby on cable. He wants the white shirts. Do you believe it? Rugby. And he wants the guys in the white shirts."

On this night, six o'clock, another night of college baskets, he is getting ready to go to work. He makes a call, then comes back and sits down at a table, a bear of a man with a stomach that looks as if he swallowed a basketball. Earlier in the day he talked with half a dozen guys around the country, an informal network built up over the years.

"You got to have a feel for it, be able to sense the hot team, the team that's coming," he says. "You got to know about the coaches, especially in the colleges, and be careful of the whistle on the road. In the pros you got to watch out for teams that lost the week before, especially early in the year, because you know they got whipped all week."

He checks his figures, power ratings he has built up over the years. Ratings based on so many points for the home court, so many points for playing two tough opponents in a row. All the variables he tries to account for. He handicaps the games himself, then checks the betting line to see if he thinks he has an edge.

"Confucius says if you want to look to the future look to the past," he says. "A lot of the same situations keep coming up year after year. Like every time URI goes to play Brown in Marvel Gym. I don't care who the players are, who the coaches are, they're always in trouble there. The figures don't lie.

"There might be only four or five good plays in a week and the key is to wait," he continues. "The average guy wants to bet a game just because it's on TV. He doesn't know how to wait. And he wants the moon in one night."

Once he used to yell and scream at the TV, kick the cat, throw a nutty when he could see a bet going down the sink. But then came the night he had a dozen games bet and he was calling all over the country trying to get the results, calling press rooms, newspapers, radio stations, eventually ending up listening to a radio report of a game over the telephone. That's when he knew that if he didn't change his act, the pace was going to kill him.

"Now I don't like to watch a game I bet on," he says. "Saves a lot of aggravation. Because you can't change the result."

He has been handicapping games for nearly 30 years, starting as a kid on a Pawtucket corner, back when he was just Anthony, not Anthony the Handicapper. That was back in the age when Rhode Island had two race tracks, a lot of action, and there was many a kid who knew what a point spread was before they ever knew their multiplication tables.

Before too long he was playing the football cards, starting to make small bets with the guy behind the candy store counter who booked some small stuff on the side. Gradually, he realized he was picking as many winners as the guys who were supposed to be good at it. That he had a certain feel for it. About 22 years ago he began handicapping full-time, a time he remembers with nostalgia. A time when he did very well on college basketball.

"Back then the bookies didn't know anything about it," he says. "Sixteen-point underdogs would win the game outright. They'd give you the wrong line. The wrong starting times. And the home courts were big then. All those little bandboxes. Places like Rodman Hall in Georgia where they used to turn off the lights. And very little of it was on TV. It was a joke."

Anthony the Handicapper remembers many of the games he made big scores on, recalling them like an old man near the end of his life, remembering past lovers. The big thing in betting then was pro football. That had started in the late '50s with the rise of the New York Giants. The games were on television, beamed into Rhode Island every Sunday, and the world was discovering the National Football League. Some say gambling made the NFL, that the rise of pro football's popularity was greatly influenced by the rise in the popularity of sports betting.

"Without gambling there would be people in the stands," says Anthony the Handicapper. "Four. The TV rating would be .01. Who would care about that second game of the doubleheader from the West Coast if you couldn't get down on it? Who would watch?"

The Super Bowl is merely a microcosm of all this. You can bet the game by the individual quarters. You can bet who scores the first touchdown. How many points are going to be scored. Anything you want.

"The whole nation's going to bet this game," says Anthony. "From the wise guys in Vegas to old ladies in nursing homes betting pennies."

Sports betting is a popularity fueled by the "Latest Line" in newspapers, and the networks' pre-game shows where guys like Jimmy the Greek - who Anthony says can't pick his nose - are as much a part of the program as the interviews. Gambling is chic now, has been for about a decade. Hollywood made movies about it like "California Split" and the "Gambler."

Then there are the touts, a profusion of sports services that sell information. The Gold Sheet, the granddaddy of sports services. The Sports Reporter. Score. The Professor. Jim Feist. Mike Warren. A whole slew of them. A couple of them are even on cable television now. Send money. Receive winners.

"Anybody who claims they can give you 80 percent winners is a liar," says Anthony. "There are a couple of good ones, guys who give you good information, but most of them are phonies. If they really could pick winners like they say they can, why are they going to tell you about it? Why not just go to Vegas and retire? What happens is you find out the same guy owns three companies and is giving out different games to everyone. Or the famous one about the guy down South who kept his phone off the hook all weekend and then said publicly he was 10-10. Some guys are so bad I want to write them a letter and tell them, 'Whatever you do, don't change, because I'm getting rich going against you.' "

Not that Anthony the Handicapper doesn't tout a few games himself. He has about a dozen guys who call him every night asking him who he likes. What he often looks for is a home underdog. Anthony likes underdogs, but only ones that he thinks can win the game outright.

"That way you have two chances to win," he says.

Traditionally, Anthony the Handicapper likes the colleges better than the pros. There are fewer teams in the pros, more people are aware of them, thus the betting line is usually more accurate. Then there's the problem in each individual sport. Pro football has too much parity. Pro basketball plays too many games ("How you supposed to know when those coke-heads want to play?" he asks). The colleges tend to play to their power ratings more. Less games. Everyone's trying.

But it's more difficult now. Freshman eligibility has made teams more of an unknown, especially early in the year. The shot clock in college basketball hurts the underdog bettor. And now everything's on TV. Games, games, and more games.

"One nut I talk to never comes out of his house," says Anthony the Handicapper. "He just sits in his house all day in his bathrobe and watches games."

He makes another call, then comes back to the table.

"I probably shouldn't play anything tonight," he says. "But sometimes I'm just like the next guy. I take a stab at something. But that's when you lose. When you get down just to have something going you might as well buy a lottery ticket. Because the average bettor loses. That's what the bookie has going for him. A bookie couldn't pick a winner if his life depended on it. He couldn't tell you the name of five guys on a team. He just takes the slips and throws them in a draw and waits for people to lose."

"But there are guys who bet every TV game just because it's on," says Anthony the Handicapper. "You can't do that and be a winner. You just got to wait. Wait for those big plums to get ripe on the tree. Then you just pick them off."

TAKE ME BACK TO LOUISQUISSET

1988

"This was golf, Rhode Island style.
Gambling and golf in the same foursome."

—Bill Reynolds

NORTH PROVIDENCE — It was called "cross-country" golf.

The players teed off from the concrete porch of the clubhouse with a putter. The object was to get to the farthest green on the course. Over greens, brooks, fairways, woods, a pond, whatever was in the way.

Cross-country golf.

It was the early '60s, at a golf course called Louisquisset in North Providence. Back then, it was a public course, one of the few public courses in the state. It also was grass-roots golf, the other side of the world away from the U.S. Open. This was golf, Rhode Island style. Gambling and golf in the same foursome.

I think back to those summers when I used to work on the course there, those last summers of my adolescence, and I see gambling and golf.

Golf and gambling.

It was a lesson I learned on my first day on the job. Out on a back fairway was a gallery of about 50 people following four golfers. Was this a tournament? What was going on? I wandered over in my 17-year-old naivete and saw money all over the green. Guys in the gallery were betting. Other guys were functioning as bookies, taking the action. There was arguing, loud voices. This was golf?

Welcome to Louisquisset.

It was one of those places that seems stuck in a time capsule, as much Rhode Island as Rocky Point, frozen lemonade, and coffee milk. One guy took numbers. He would be walking down one fairway and someone would yell a number at him and he would wave back and make a notation in his notepad. One guy sold "hot" suits from the trunk of his car. Guys were always playing cards in the clubhouse, or else putting for money on the practice green in front of the small clubhouse.

Guys were always arguing, loud voices drifting over the emerald green fairways. Someone always was throwing a club. Or in the woods looking for balls. Or trying to fish a ball out of a brook. Or trying to kick the ball into a better lie when no one was looking. Or shanking some shot off to the right. Everyone seemed to have a nickname. Little Joe. John the Bomb. Louie the Whip. Knobby. Tiny.

It was all a long way from the golf you see on television, the golf of the country club swings and the picture-postcard courses, the golf of the U.S. Open.

Etiquette?

That was just another word in the dictionary no one knew how to spell.

There were few caddies. There were mats to tee off from instead of grass. There was little rough. Everything was geared to get the golfers through the course as quickly as possible. My job essentially was to cut greens, and by the second summer I knew the routine. The rule of thumb was simple: Don't stop. If guys were on the green, keep cutting anyway.

"Hey buddy," some guy would invariably say. "Turn that off, will ya?"

"Hey buddy," I'd snap back. "What is this? The Open. You putt and I'll cut."

Weekends we had to start cutting greens at 5 a.m., so the course would be ready by first light. Sometimes my brother and I stayed up all night, arrived in the murky darkness, driving his car onto the course and cutting greens by headlights. By 6 in the morning, the golfers were lined up on the first tee. For this was the early '60s. Golf was exploding in popularity, courtesy of Arnold Palmer and Sunday afternoon telecasts of the PGA Tour. No longer was it merely a country club game. The long waits on the tee every weekend were testimony to that. These were the weekend golfers, the Saturday morning hackers pulling their carts, just like at any other public course, their golf balls rolling through the early-morning dew.

But it was the gamblers during the week that made Louisquisset unique. In a sense, they had made it their own private club. They hung around the clubhouse all morning, arranging their games for the afternoon, along with side bets on the putting green. Afternoons they played for money, tense matches as dramatic as anything you see at the Open, their loud voices drifting over the quiet fairways.

And the best event was "cross country" golf. Teeing off the porch with a putter. All heading for the 16th green on the far side of the course. Having to go over the 18th green. The ninth fairway. The fifth. The sixth. The eighth. Then over the pond and up to the 16th green that sat on the side of a slight hill underneath a big, shady, tree.

Condos now stand where the 16th green used to be, and it's been years since Louisquisset operated as a public course. Who knows where the gamblers have ended up? Through the years I have heard snippets of information. This guy did a little time for interstate gambling. That guy got pinched for something else. This guy had become one of the biggest bookies in the state. That guy died. Like the unofficial newsletter from some alumni club.

Now those long-ago summers back at Louisquisset belong to a different place. But it all came rushing back at me this past weekend at the U.S. Open in Brookline. For three days I watched the best players in the world play almost flawless golf, booming drives, crisp irons, the whole enchilada. Three days of watching golf that looks as if it was programmed by some computer jock. And after a while there was a part of me that wished someone would throw a club, or have a temper tantrum, kick a ball out of the rough. I started hoping someone would shank a shot, do something familiar.

Because to me the Open is not real golf. Great golf, yes. Real golf, no. Real golf is what they used to play at Louisquisset. Back when they used to tee off the concrete porch with a putter and play cross-country.

AS FANS GO, HE'S THE WORST—OR THE BEST

1988

"What else do you want me to do?
Stay home and watch TV?"

—Carl Koussa

KINGSTON — Let's see.

He has hitchhiked to West Virginia and been to games in Hawaii, Miami and San Francisco, not to mention Orono, Maine. He has been thrown out of the gym at the University of Massachusetts for starting a mini-riot in the stands, and once was chased through the ice and snow at the University of New Hampshire by a group of football players who didn't particularly like his vociferous cheering.

He once sneaked out of the student infirmary to see a game, and has been known to pound his fist against walls and smash windshields after losses. After some especially difficult losses, he's felt physically sick for three or four days, unable to eat or sleep. He has kept scrapbooks on every season for 20 years. Last year, he says, he spent nearly one-third of his salary to attend games.

Oh yeah. He also has not missed a home basketball game at the University of Rhode Island for 23 years. Not one. In fact, he says he's only missed about 11 Ram games in those 23 years, and currently has a streak of 68 in a row.

Meet Carl Koussa, my vote for the number one, all-time,

first-ballot-Hall-of-Fame, Rhode Island basketball sicko. Number one. All-time.

The first time I remember seeing him was the first year URI played in the Civic Center in the early 70's, when he literally came out of the stands, walked on the court and began yelling at the referee. At the time I thought it was just an aberration.

Little did I know.

Now he has become part of URI basketball. He is everywhere. He is in the lobby before games. He is in arguments at halftime. He is in the locker room after games. Last year when the Rams played in Madison Square Garden, where security is tight, he got back where the locker rooms are by saying he was the brother of the coach, Tommy Penders.

If you go to a URI game and don't see Koussa, you aren't looking.

"What else do you want me to do?" he says. "Stay home and watch TV? Walk around my apartment in circles? I'm not married, so URI basketball is my wife."

His obsession started innocently enough.

That was back in the mid-'60s when he was attending high school in Central Falls. Several of his friends were on the basketball team and he began going to the team's games. All the games.

His older brother Harold was a student at URI at the time, and one night, Koussa went to a game in Kingston. The Rams played a St. Bonaventure team that featured Bob Lanier in a sold-out Keaney Gym. It was the era of Steve Chubin and Art Stephenson at URI, an exciting time, and for Koussa it was like love at first sight, a sports version of "Some Enchanted Evening." He loved the team. The crowd. The excitement. All of it.

"I was overwhelmed," he says. "I was in awe."

His grand passion had begun.

While a student at URI he sat right behind the opposing bench and berated the coach and players alike with a steady stream of invectives. How bad was he?

"I was worse than brutal," he says quickly. "UMass coach Jackie Leaman once said I was a five-point advantage for URI."

Now he thinks nothing of driving to Philadelphia for a game. Once he drove his car off the road in a snowstorm on his way to a game in Olean, N.Y. He loves to fly around the country with the Rams. ("I get on the plane and start hitting on the stewardess. I don't let up until she agrees to go out with me.") And it doesn't matter what kind of season the Rams are having. The year they went 6-22 he only missed one game.

Long ago, URI basketball became more than just games to him. It became a way of life. The people. The friendships. The entire subculture. He knows all the players, talks to many of them on the phone.

In a sense the games have become his social life. When URI is not playing he goes to any game he can find near his apartment in suburban Hartford, where he runs a company that finds jobs for engineers. College games. High school games. Any game. Usually, five or six nights a week throughout the winter.

And he always gets in. Long ago he made an art form out of getting into sold-out games. He carries a phony press pass that identifies him as a "basketball scout," and he claims he can talk his way into any game. The trick is to "dress well, act important, and always park right in front of the building no matter what the sign says."

Last week he went to see UConn play in Storrs. The game was sold out. He had no ticket.

Do you really think he didn't get in?

"Going to a game is like picking up a girl and going out on a date," he says, his voice growing more animated. "That's what a game is to me. I get high every game. I get a rush. I'm addicted and probably will be the rest of my life. People don't understand. I have to go to URI games. Why do people eat? Why do people sleep? URI basketball is a part of my daily normal being."

The key word in that last sentence is "normal."

The last few years he's often been joined by his brother Steve, who goes 6-foot-5, 298 pounds and runs a fitness center in Narragansett. Last year at San Diego State, when a group of kids were heckling the Rams, Steve Koussa walked over to one of them and ripped the jacket off his back. End of heckling.

"When the URI players get yelled at, it is like we are being yelled at," says Carl Koussa. "It hurts me, and my brother."

And now it's starting again. Another season in a long-running affair that began one night in Keaney Gym many years ago. Another season in the life of the all-time, first-ballot-Hall-of-Fame, URI basketball sicko.

"I've loved all of it," he says, his voice low and wistful, like a man at the end of his life remembering old lovers. "I just wish everyone could see basketball the way Carl Koussa looks at it."

WORST GAME TURNS INTO THE BEST

1988

"Just once. Just once and I'll never ask for anything again."
—Georgina Knox

CENTRAL FALLS — His idea had been to pick the worst high school football game he could find.

On a Saturday when college football danced on the national stage, and the best high school teams were on display across the state, the Sports Writer's idea had been to find the flip side of all this excitement, a game out of some football netherworld.

And what better school to watch than Ponaganset, whose teams had lost 26 games in a row, Rhode Island's answer to Columbia? Ponaganset, which had gone more than two seasons without a victory?

So yesterday morning the Sports Writer was at Macomber Stadium for Ponaganset at Central Falls, and in the beginning everything seemed according to script. A brown-and-white factory bordered one side of the field. Behind one end zone, off in the distance, was a red-brick factory. Behind the other were train tracks. Everything looked as grim as some Dickens' novel, the Industrial Revolution in decline.

There was no scoreboard, few bleachers. About 50 people waited for the game to start. There were no benches for the players. Fifteen spectators were on the Ponaganset side. The Sports Writer stood on the sidelines feeling smug. It doesn't get any more small-time than this, he told himself. He had come to the right place. A football netherworld.

Then it got more complicated.

From the beginning the Ponaganset team showed remarkable spirit. The reserves yelled encouragement to their teammates. The entire team erupted in a burst of emotion when they scored the first touchdown, taking a 7-0 lead. The Sports Writer was surprised. He had been around many bad teams, where losing cast its long pall, and the air smelled like failure. Bad teams where everyone was just going through the motions, all but mailing the losses in, secretly praying for the season to end.

This was different. If at first glance this was just another game in a season where the cheers always were somewhere else, it was being played with all the intensity of kids on a mission. The Sports Writer had come looking for some game played on football's nowhere ward. He hadn't expected this.

"Why?" he asked a woman standing next to him. "Why do they have such great spirit?"

"I think it's because they're all friends," she said. "They get down, but they always seem to pick each other up. And even afterwards, when they lose, they blame themselves, not each other."

Her name is Georgianna Knox, and she is the mother of one of the players. She also is one of the forgotten people of high school sports, one of those parents who picks the kids up after practice, goes to all the games, lives and dies a thousand deaths on the sidelines, cares as much as the kids.

"But it's tough for them because no one goes to the games," she said. "If we get 50 people, we're lucky. Last week was our homecoming and when the cheerleaders yelled, 'Give us a "P," ' one person yelled back."

The score was 14-6 at halftime, Ponaganset ahead. For their halftime talk, the players went behind the end zone and sat in the grass. But they had been up at halftime two other times this year, only to see it all fall apart in the second half, the losing streak growing. Chris Branch, the second-year Ponaganset coach who has never won a game, was telling them to keep playing aggressively, not to let up.

"One more half," yelled a guy in a green coat as the team came back for the second half. "It's all yours. Take it."

The Sports Writer continued to stand on the sidelines and watch. But no longer was he the detached observer, there to chronicle another day of futility. He could feel himself being caught up in the emotion, once more becoming aware that sometimes sports don't get any better than when played by high school kids who play for all the right reasons.

If he had come looking for the worst game he could find, here he was watching a high school team that only has known failure fighting for some self-respect. Here he was watching a team that had every reason to have quit a long time ago, but was showing that sports is all about second effort and not giving up, and all those things that sound so corny until you see them before your eyes on a Saturday morning.

Was sports any better than this?

He didn't think so.

Central Falls took the second-half kickoff and started driving. To Ponaganset's 30. To the 20. To the 5. It all seemed inevitable. Central Falls was going to score, the momentum was changing. But penalties stopped the Central Falls drive, and Ponaganset was still in the lead. The third quarter ended. Twelve minutes away.

"Just once," said Georgianna Knox, the anxiety in her voice. "Just once and I'll never ask for anything again. But I'm already so proud of these kids. We've never been this close before."

"All those days in the rain," said the woman next to her, rubbing her hands together, no doubt running all those futile afternoons through her mind, all 26 of them.

"You can do it," yelled a cheerleader in a green-and-white uniform, her voice almost pleading.

Four minutes to play, Ponaganset holding on, tension on the sideline, seconds ticked away as slowly as time through the hour glass. Central Falls got the ball back, but an intercepted pass gave Ponaganset the ball again. They made a first down. Then another. The seconds kept ticking, the players on the sidelines sensing it, feeling it get close.

And when it was over, and Ponaganset had won, the players jumped all over themselves in a joyous celebration, Georgianna Knox had tears in her eyes, and Chris Branch fell to his knees, lost in some private moment. Later he would say he couldn't believe it; that all week he had told his team to play with pride. To forget the losing streak, and all the negatives that went with it, and just go play football.

The Sports Writer walked off the field and crossed the street near the yellow Ponaganset bus. The players already were in the bus, a study in pandemonium. Someone poured a bottle of champagne over Branch's head, just like they do in the big games on television. The Sports Writer watched the bus go down the street past the brown and white factory and knew that no team in the country was going to be any happier on this day than this Ponaganset football team. And as he watched the bus turn the corner and disappear from view, the Sports Writer also knew that sometimes you find the essence of sports in the strangest places.

His idea had been to pick the worst high school football game he could find.

THE DOWN AND DIRTY POLO CLUB

1989

"We don't yell at each other for making a mistake. We fist fight."

—Raymond Jenkins

PROVIDENCE — Let's see. Where do we start?

Is it that they've been known to fight among themselves on the softball field in the middle of a game, two teammates actually throwing punches at each other?

Is it that they have been known to butt heads to get each other psyched up?

Or that they are notorious for yelling at each other during games, occurrences that happen seemingly as often as ground balls to the shortstop?

Is it that they're infamous for yelling at umpires, cursing at fans, and just generally being the bad boys of Neutaconkanut Park? Or that in the world of local softball, there is nothing like the Polo Club, a team from Federal Hill that brings new meaning to having a passion for the game?

"If I have to run into the backstop and split my head open to catch a ball, I won't think twice," says Sergio Scarcella, a short stocky guy who founded the team about eight years ago, after some of the older guys on Federal Hill wouldn't let him and his buddies play. "I will run into a wall and not think nothing about it. That's what I'm going to do. That's what we expect. And if you don't do it, you might get slapped by a couple of us after the game."

"How important is softball?" Wayne Durante asks. "It's so

important that if we don't win I don't sleep with my wife. I won't even stay in the same room with her I'm so upset. There is nothing as important as this, and my wife knows it."

It is Wednesday night and the Polos are standing in front of the section of wooden bleachers at this ball yard in Silver Lake minutes before they are going to play Sports Cafe. They are wearing their white Polo uniforms with the powder blue trim, the ones with the insignia of a polo player on it, the ultimate preppie symbol. So, what is this Federal Hill softball team, which admits to getting crazy once it gets on the field, doing wearing prepped out polo gear?

"I'm a big Ralph Lauren fan," says Sergio Scarcella, matter-of-factly.

Ralph Lauren?

Somehow it's a little difficult seeing Ralph Lauren in the lineup. Scarcella even once wrote to the company, wondering if Ralph Lauren wanted to sponsor the team. He never got an answer. No matter. The Polo Club operates by itself, raising the entry fee itself, independent. They like it that way. Like the people yelling at them, and the league officials who sometimes are embarrassed by them, and some of the umpires who think the Polos try to intimidate them. Like the fact they are the bad boys. Like the fact that no one quite knows what to make of them.

Because, to them, being a member of the Polo Club is the ultimate. Not even family gets in the way. There are three Scarcellas on the team, but one time one of their cousins was on the team and just wasn't cutting it. So they sent him a pink slip through the mail telling him his days as a Polo were over. Sentiment is for suckers. They may all be guys from the neighborhood, growing up together, playing together, year after year, even having their vanity license plates with "POLO" on them, but once the game starts, all that's forgotten. It's win or else.

"We don't yell at each other for making a mistake," says

Raymond Jenkins, a stocky blond guy with a scar that runs down his left cheek. "We fist fight."

"We head-butt each other," says Sergio Scarcella. "We have to yell, swear, scream, holler. And if you don't hustle, you get slapped. Afterwards, it's all forgotten. But we think nothing of seeing two guys go head-to-head in the middle of a game."

The game is about to start. It is nearing 9:30. Bugs circle around the light tower. Some teenage girls with oh-so-tough looks on their faces sashay by. A few dozen people sit in the small grandstand in back of the third-base line. A few others are in the wooden bleachers behind the first-base bench. Softball, Rhode Island style. Save the glamour for somewhere else.

The Polo Club gathers in a huddle on the dirt in front of its bench. They start yelling, their voices blending together in a roar. "ONE, TWO, THREE, POLO," they shout, then run out on the field, their shoes raising dust in the skinned infield. Maybe not quite as dramatic as a team in Massachusetts famous for rolling around in the dirt before the game starts, but effective nonetheless.

"When the game starts people know we're there," says Scarcella's brother, Guliano, with a knowing smile.

By the bottom of the third inning, the Polo Club is down 4-0, and you would think the sky is about to fall. There is no joy in Mudville. The Polos again gather in a huddle, their voices urgent, pleading.

"I'm so ashamed to be a member of this team," says Jenkins, his voice near distress. "What's going on here? I'm so ashamed."

A few minutes later, a Polo Club runner is on first.

"Yo, Anthony," Jenkins yells to the runner. "Take that guy out on the double play. I want to see dirt on your face."

The Polos come back and tie the score. The see-saw of emotion they have been on for the first three innings is now tilted toward elation. It's short-lived, however. Sports Cafe goes ahead 7-4 in the top of the fourth, and once again the Polos seem on the brink of despair as they come to their bench in the bottom of the inning.

"We're playin' like a bunch of GIRLS," yells Jenkins. "We should have sent our sistahs. Come on, we got to start playing like MEN. Be aggressive. That's our style."

When an outfielder from Sports Cafe makes a diving catch and the umpire signals an out, the Polos run out on the field in protest.

"It came out of his glove as big as a bowling ball," shouts Jenkins. "You could have knocked down pins with that."

"Come on, blue," yells Sergio Scarcella, on the field, hands on his hips, glaring at the umpire. "Call them right."

The umpire appears unfazed. The umpires are used to the Polo Club. This is just a minor protest.

It's also merely the start of more frustration for the Polos. Going into the bottom of the fifth they are down 9-4, not a good sign in a seven-inning game. The summer air is full of four-letter words. Gloves are thrown into the dirt. Someone yells to someone else about missing a cutoff man. Someone else is admonished for hitting a fly ball. Fear and loathing in the on-deck circle.

"I can't believe this," screams Durante to no one in particular.

"What are we going to do, quit?" says John Duffy. "Give up? Go home now?"

You know Duffy's not going to do that. Not someone who postponed his wedding this summer because it conflicted with a softball game. In the wooden bleachers sits Durante's wife Mary. She knows the score.

"Believe me, if they don't win, we suffer," she says.

On the field the Polos get two runs. They are now down 9-6 going into the bottom of the sixth, and things don't look good. Every player who makes an out returns to the bench enveloped in gloom. Some of the guys keep right on running past first base to the wire fence along right field and stand there for a second, alone with their sense of failure.

Durante does a belly slide across home plate to narrow Sports Cafe's lead to 9-7. The Polos get two more runs and tie it. Pandemonium at Neutaconkanut Park.

"We're MEN now," yells Jenkins as the Polos hug each other and slap wrists.

Jenkins steps into the batter's box, all fire and determination. But Sports Cafe decides to intentionally walk him.

"No," he wails. "Have some heart. You can't do this to me. Don't let this happen."

Shortly afterward, the Polos again go down a run. Again, they come back to tie the game in the bottom of the inning. This time Durante hits a triple to deep left, scoring Jackie Poulios, and slides face first into third. The Polos charge onto the field as if they had just won the American League pennant. The umpire finally gets them to clear the field so the game can continue.

Extra innings.

There is no scoring in the eighth. Then, in the bottom of the ninth, it's the Polos' turn, and they can sense victory.

"I can't wait to get muckled at the plate," says Anthony Massarone.

"Jesus ain't knocking me over," says Jenkins.

The air is charged with anticipation. The last inning of the American League pennant? This is the same feeling to the Polos. For softball is their major league, Neutaconkanut is their Fenway, and this is their moment.

The Polos load the bases with one out, and Durante is up. The Polos are all but dancing in the dirt. Durante lofts the ball into the outfield, the runner tags up at third, the game is over. The Polo Club celebrates in the infield. Let the devil take tomorrow. The Polos are now in second place, and all is right in their little corner of the world.

TOM ECCLESTON KEEPS BURRILLVILLE'S TRADITION ALIVE

1988

"They all know who Mr. Eccleston is. The stories have been passed down."

—Bill Mandigo

BURRILLVILLE — You come here looking for the past.

You come in winter, and that is important because once upon a time this was a town that seemed to live for winter. Hockey was the town's lifeblood then, the glue that brought all the old mill villages together. It was all a wonderful fairy tale then, the amazing story of the little school in the middle of nowhere that kept winning championships.

Every winter, back then, there seemed to be more young kids skating into the old Rhode Island Auditorium in Providence in their rag-tag clothes. Almost as if it were a crusade. They would come down from the north country in their floppy socks and their blue uniforms that didn't always match, the skates that seemed like they had seen too many frozen ponds. They would skate onto the ice in that old cavernous building on North Main Street, cheered on by their hordes of fans who viewed the trip down to Providence as a pilgrimage, and invariably skate circles around all the kids in their pressed uniforms and fancy equipment.

Year after year.

It is a time forever bathed in a soft orange light for Burrillville, a magical time. The little school that became one of the key names in New England high school hockey. They were Horatio Alger on skates, a scriptwriter's dream. Even now, so many years later, to anyone who came of age in Rhode Island a generation ago, Burrillville always will be schoolboy hockey. Did they really used to skate from September to May? Did they really use to practice on outdoor ponds all over town, following the ice from pond to pond? Who really knew? But after a while it all became part of the legend, the fiction sprinkled in with the truth.

Now you come here and everything's changed.

You come on a winter's day, through the fields covered with snow, past the old mills that are monuments to another era, past the new homes that are starting to turn this old mill town into another suburb. If once the high school was in the middle of Harrisville, an old red brick building that seemed to come direct from Central Casting, now the school is newer, suburban, down the road from some condos. If once the hockey team practiced on frozen ponds, now there is a rink out behind the high school. If once hockey seemed right up there with death and taxes in importance here, now, in many ways, it's just another sport. Still important, mind you. But no longer the crusade it once was.

But it is here, in this rink with blue walls, where the past and the present intersect. For here on the rink, dressed all in blue and coaching high school kids, is 77-year-old Tom Eccleston, the man who started it all, so many years ago.

Three years ago Tom Eccleston came back to chase his own myth. Not that he really set out to do it.

He had retired from the Hill School in Pennsylvania and came back to this small northern Rhode Island town where he first had come in 1934, this town that long ago had become home for him. At the time he thought coaching was all behind him. After all, he was 75, and there had been a lot of teams, a lot of games, since coaching had started for him back in the Depression.

But times had changed for Burrillville hockey. The glory days were in the past tense, memories, and in a sense the past was staring down on the present like an accuser. There had been three coaches in the last decade. Three local guys who all had decided the criticism and second-guessing wasn't worth it. So Eccleston was asked to coach again. Dust off the myth, and get back on the ice, the old patriarch trying to put Humpty-Dumpty back together again.

"No one wanted it," he says. "It wasn't like I had to beat out a lot of competition."

At the time it became a national story. Here was this 75-year-old man who had come back to coach at the school where he had started the hockey team nearly 50 years before. Burrillville's answer to Mr. Chips. USA Today came. Yankee Magazine came. Even CBS. Who could resist the story of this 75-year-old prodigal son? Then at the end of the year he took Burrillville to a state title, its first one in years. Making it a little more Hollywood was that they won it with 42 seconds to go in double overtime. You couldn't have asked for a better story.

Now it's two years later and the national media has gone and Eccleston is still here. He's 77 now, but he still comes down here to this rink most every noontime to skate. He plays in two hockey leagues. And he's still coaching, after all these years.

"The thing is I always thought of myself as a football coach," he says with a smile.

For Eccleston never set out to be a hockey coach. He never even played hockey formally. He spent his last high school years at Moses Brown in Providence, where there was no hockey team at the time. At Brown he played soccer. He got out in 1932, the middle of the Depression, unsure about his future. The only thing he was sure of was he didn't want to go to work in the Greenville mill where his father was superintendent. So he hitched on for a while with a tramp freighter to South America. When he came back, he was offered a job teaching the sixth grade in the Georgiaville section of North Providence.

As he remembers it, he had no clue how to teach.

"I don't know anything about teaching art," he told the superintendent.

"Bring in some fruit and have the kids draw it," the superintendent said.

"I don't know anything about teaching music."

"Here's a pitch pipe," the superintendent said.

The birth of a career.

He had 50 students and only 40 seats. He improvised. The next year he went to Burrillville to be a teacher and football coach. There were 18 mills in the town then, scattered around the villages of Pascoag, Harrisville, Nasonville, Oakland, Mapleville. It was in the northwestern tip of the state, isolated, a world unto itself, a world that revolved around the mills.

Soon afterwards, he introduced hockey. Not that there was any real plan to it. Nothing formal. After football season he got a few kids together, they found a pond. No big deal. He used to skate with them. One of the kids on that first team was Babe Mousseau, who later would succeed him as coach and keep the tradition going. At the end of the year, they played an unofficial game against Pomfret Academy because he had a friend that coached there. He had 15 kids.

For the first three years they played only one game a year. Then they finally joined the Interscholastic League. The second year they went to the state finals, and the legend started. How every kid had to bring 12 feet of board to build a rink every year, the one pre-requisite for being on the team. How they practiced on ponds. How every once in awhile some kid would fall through the ice.

What has gotten lost in the legend was that Eccleston also was one of the most successful schoolboy football and baseball coaches the state has ever seen. His football teams only lost six league games in 19 years, once won 26 games in a row. His baseball teams once won three state championships in a row.

But it was in hockey that he made his state-wide reputation by turning Burrillville into one of the most famous hockey names in New England. It was in hockey where he was the architect of an athletic fantasy. And right from the beginning, regardless of the sport, his own rule was that no kid ever got cut, and everyone got into at least two games, no matter what. It was a legacy of his own experience as a high school football player in Maine.

"I remember how much it meant to me once in high school football to get into a game," he says. "It meant everything to me."

For Eccleston never had been much of an athlete himself.

"But I loved athletics as a kid and the only way I could play was if I organized the team."

He also always seemed to have a knack for knowing how to get kids to respond. Mousseau told the story of how he once was in the eighth grade in Pascoag, already becoming hard to handle, when his teacher asked Eccleston to speak to him. Eccleston didn't know who Mousseau was, but he told Mousseau he'd seen him playing football in Pascoag and that he was a natural. But that if he wanted to play next year at the high school he had to reform. He also told Mousseau he'd be watching him. The next year, Mousseau was an instant star.

After his freshman year in high school, Mousseau approached Eccleston and said he was quitting school. He had played high school football and now it was time to go work in the mill.

"But you can't quit," said Eccleston. "Because next year we are going to win the championship and you want to be around for that, don't you?"

He stayed. Burrillville won the championship. Then Mousseau decided again to quit school.

"You can't quit now, Babe," Eccleston said, "because the team just elected you captain."

Already, Eccleston had become larger than life in Burrillville. It was a different time, a time when the high school coach was the most respected person in town, part mentor, part surrogate father, revered. A time when a coach's words were almost chiseled in stone. Eccleston coached football, hockey, baseball. He became the principal of the high school, later the superintendent. To the rest of the state, he was Burrillville.

Mousseau replaced Eccleston as the Burrillville hockey coach in 1957, not only keeping the tradition alive, but adding to it. Eccleston went on to coach at Providence College where he was national coach of the year in 1964. In 1971 he went to teach and coach at the Hill School in Pennsylvania. He was 61 years old.

Sixteen years later, the rink echoes with the sounds of the puck into the boards, the crunching of skates into the ice, an occasional whistle. Eccleston is out on the ice, skating back and forth, giving advice, encouragement. He is coaching. A few minutes later the team starts filing off the ice, all these kids who were born after Eccleston left Burrillville to go to the Hill School; these kids who are the same age as his grandchildren.

But if nothing else is the same as it was back when Eccleston used to be the Burrillville hockey coach, he still coaches the same. He still disciplines the same. He still teaches fundamental hockey, complete with a 66-page playbook. He still gets nervous on game day. The years have come and gone, the whole world has changed, but Eccleston always has thought of himself as a teacher first. Maybe that's something that has never gone out of style.

And what of these Burrillville kids who now are coming of age in such a different time?

"They all know who Mr. Eccleston is," says Bill Mandigo, the junior varsity coach. "The stories have been passed down."

On the wall of the rink is a sign that reminds you of the tradition. How Burrillville has won 14 state titles, five New England titles. The glorious tradition that once upon a time seemed to be a fairy tale, a gone forever time that even now, so many years later, seems bathed in a soft orange light.

But you really don't need the sign to tell you of the past. Not really. All you have to do on this winter afternoon is look out on the rink and see this 77-year-old man skating with his team, the past and the present on the same rink.

TOMMY ARRUDA'S SECOND ACT

1988

"There's something about this city.
You go away and you always come back."

—TOMMY ARRUDA

FALL RIVER — The man who might just be the greatest athlete in Fall River history is sitting across the street from Kennedy Park on this July morning, the sun already beating down like an accuser. There is no one in the park except for an elderly man in suspenders who walks by himself on a distant field.

"When we were kids you had to get here by 9 in the morning or you didn't get to play," says Tom Arruda. "Now . . ."

His voice trails off.

Arruda is the coach of the Spindle City American Legion team, but this story is not really about that. Instead, it is about the other side of a baseball career. It's been 17 years since Tommy Arruda decided to call it quits, nearly two decades since he tabled his dream of one day playing in the big leagues. Seventeen years since he came back to Fall River, came home.

And it also is, in a sense, about giving something back.

Once upon a time Tommy Arruda was a prodigy of sorts, a two-sport star at Durfee High School, all-New England in basketball, trailed by scouts in baseball. It was 1958, and the world was a different place. It was a time of bonus babies, a time of tryouts. He worked out at Ebbets Field, Yankee Stadium, the Polo Grounds, pitching on the sidelines. Eight teams offered him contracts, and he went over to Magoni's Restaurant, over the bridge in Somerset, and signed with the Giants for $4,000, big money for a kid who grew up "below the hill," a Fall River euphemism for growing up poor.

That first year he went off to Michigan City Indiana, Class D, life in the bushes. Two dollars and fifty cents a day meal money.

"To me, it was paradise," he says.

He was 18-8 that year. The next year it was Fresno. Then Tacoma. Later it was Oklahoma City and Springfield and Buffalo and Rochester and God knows where else. Once he rode a bus for 42 hours between Texas and Vera Cruz, Mexico. One time in Tacoma, in Triple-A, he struck out 11 Giants in five innings in an exhibition game. Then Willie Mays came up and hit one halfway up the mountain in back of the outfield fence.

He was with the Giants' organization for eight years, then was bought by Houston, then traded to Baltimore. Along the way he was teammates with Juan Marichal and Gaylord Perry. He roomed with Jim Palmer. He pitched against Tommy John and both Niekros, brothers Phil and Joe. He played for Earl Weaver when the Earl was in Triple-A in Rochester, often going to the race track with him.

And he came close to getting to the big leagues.

Oh, how he came close.

He went to spring training four times with Baltimore. In 1966, with the Astros, the last roster spot came down to him and Robin Roberts, then in the twilight of a great career. One year when the Orioles needed a pitcher, they called up Wally Bunker from Rochester, even though Arruda was pitching better at the time.

And he always loved the life. The endless bus rides. The cramped locker rooms. The uncertainty. The travel. Life on the road. All of it. For he was making a living playing ball, and what was any better than that for a kid from "below the hill"? And until he was 29, he always thought he was going to get to the major leagues.

But by 1971 he was with the Twins' organization and he knew he never was going to get to the big leagues. He had a family by then, and there had been too many summers where he had gone off to chase his dream, a dream that had started to recede in the distance, had gotten out of reach. So he came home, back to the magnet that is Fall River.

"I don't know," he says, "there's something about this city. You go away and you always come back."

Not that there wasn't a big adjustment.

He had been in the minor leagues 13 years, and now he had to enter Act II of his life. For a while baseball was something he was trying to push into the past. Guys wanted him to play in leagues around the area, but he said no, thanks. He had been so close, and even to this day he's not sure why he didn't make it. Politics? Image? The fact he always seemed to be wearing blue jeans and cut-off T-shirts? Wrong place, wrong time?

Who really knows.

"I always wanted to pitch just one game in the big leagues," he says wistfully, like a man who yearns for just one more adolescent summer. "Just one."

Then one day he got involved coaching his son's Little League team. Then he started a Pony League team in Fall River. Then he went out and hustled some money and resurrected a defunct American Legion team.

That was 10 years ago.

He is 48 now, and his real job is working for the city as a painter. But he coaches both Spindle City, one of two Legion teams in the city, and a Little League team. He has become one of the people who keep the game alive in Fall River, someone who went away a long time ago to chase his own dream and then came back to be one of the dream-weavers, one of those people in every town who give up their time and a piece of themselves to help kids.

And maybe making it even more special is that once Tommy Arruda was one of the great ones in Fall River, someone whose exploits bought him a little slice of immortality in the city's folklore.

1990-1999

Johnny Most, courtesy of Boston Sports Museum

MEMORIES OF JOHNNY MOST STEAL THE SHOW

1990

"This is Johnny Most high above courtside here in the Boston Garden."

BOSTON — It doesn't seem the same, of course.

You turn on the Celtics games on the radio now and there is no Johnny Most, his raspy voice the product of too many cigarettes and too many late nights in too many faraway hotels, looking at the world through a green lens. No references to "tricky dribbling" or "fiddling and diddling," expressions that Most long ago turned into a trademark.

No "McFilthy and McNasty." No villains.

He still does the pregame show, but now Glenn Ordway broadcasts the games and somehow it's not the same. Not like all the times when Most started his broadcast by saying, "This is Johnny Most high above courtside here in the Boston Garden, where the Celtics are about to do basketball battle." An introduction that came to symbolize Celtic basketball for over 35 years.

Like the time he opened up a broadcast in Atlanta by saying, "I hate Atlanta. They stole my wallet." Or when he came on the air in Portland saying, "The fans have to take a number when they come through the turnstiles because they are animals." All this in a voice bordering on hysteria.

And if you grew up in New England and were a Celtics fan, you grew up listening to Johnny Most. Grew up with "Jungle Jim" and "Wilt the Stilt," with "Roughhouse Rudy" and "Jarrin' John, the Bouncing Buckeye from Ohio State," all the nicknames that became part of Most's personal signature on a game. His call of "Havlicek stole the ball]" is forever lodged in New England history, the basketball equivalent of "The Redcoats are coming]"

You also grew up with the recognition that the basketball world was a hostile place, full of people who wanted to harm the Celtics. You soon learned Most's broadcast version of history, one never burdened by the truth.

Some of that was a product of the times. He began broadcasting the Celtics games in 1953, at a time when the Celtics were little more than an afterthought on the Boston sports scene, back when Most was also expected to dramatize things, as much pitchman as broadcaster. No one had to tell him twice. Johnny always understood it's all theater.

It's a style that endured, even as everything else around him changed. For he always has belonged to another time, Johnny Most has. A time when the locker rooms always were too small and there never was enough hot water to go around. Back when the NBA was little more than a barnstorming league, professional wrestling in sneakers, complete with heroes and villains, the good guys and the bad guys.

Johnny Most embodied all that. He was direct from Central Casting, complete with the voice everyone has always tried to imitate and the face that belonged on Mount Rushmore, all creases and crevices, as if every Celtic is etched there.

"I wasn't born," he once quipped. "Damon Runyon created me."

Who could argue?

It was all part of his uniqueness. Love him or hate him, but understand one thing. There never will be anyone else like him.

AH, TONY C AND ME, BACK WHEN WE WERE 19

1990

"I have had good times in the past, and I know I will have good times again in the future."

—Tony Conigliaro

PROVIDENCE — He's been dead more than a week now, but I still can't shake the image of that day in April, 1964, when I first heard of Tony Conigliaro.

I was in a school in Worcester then, and it wasn't a real good time for me. I had just turned 19, my long-time girlfriend was in the process of dumping me, and that realization had become an ache in my heart. I had hitchhiked into Boston and spent the afternoon sitting in a student apartment, drinking beers and feeling sorry for myself. Everyone was talking about the "Boston Strangler," the serial killer who was terrorizing the city.

On the radio was the ball game, the Red Sox home opener. It was the debut of Conigliaro, the local kid. I had never heard of him. Someone said he had hit a home run in his first time at bat in Fenway Park. He was 19.

I remember sitting there thinking about how different our lives were. Here we were the same age, yet he was hitting a home run in Fenway Park in his first time at bat, and I was sitting in a seedy apartment with my world coming apart. On that spring afternoon, in my particular view of the universe, Tony Conigliaro was everything I was not.

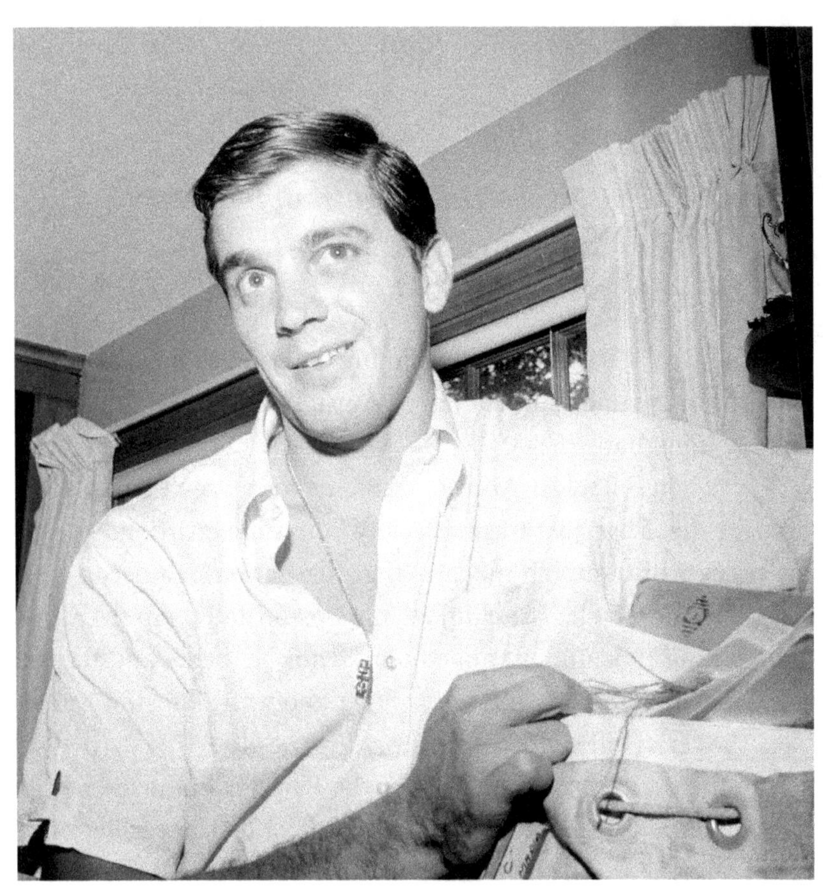

Courtesy of Boston Sports Museum

So began a curious kinship.

Maybe it was because my first childhood dream had been to be a baseball player, to play in Fenway Park for the Red Sox. Maybe it was because Conigliaro was living out every New England kid's fantasy. Maybe it was something more elusive, undefinable, the little-understood reasons why we identify with certain athletes and not with others. The mysterious reasons why we cheer for some, while others touch our hearts.

For the next few years I always would look in the box score to see how Tony C. did. Not that I was really a baseball fan. Certainly not as I had been when a kid. Baseball had become something stowed away in that footlocker labeled childhood. I followed the Red Sox only in the most peripheral of ways, a game here and there.

Except for Tony C.

He became a link to the baseball of my youth. In some strange way his success became my success. If he was doing well, then things seemed a little more right. As if in my mind our fates had become linked together that April day in 1964, when we both were 19.

It wasn't his celebrity I was attracted to. Or that he had become a certifiable New England hero, bigger than Yaz back then. It was because we were both the same age. And once upon a time we had come to Boston on the same day, he to begin his major-league career with the Red Sox, me to get dumped by a girlfriend who had been the center of my little world. No one ever said that being a fan has to make sense.

The day after he got hit in the face by Jack Hamilton in that Impossible Dream summer of 1967, there was a picture of Tony C. in a Boston paper. Even now, so many years later, I vividly recall it. The incredibly swollen eye. The deep bruise. The forlorn look on his face.

The other thing I remember was his quote.

"I have had good times in the past," he said from his hospital bed, "and I know I will have good times again in the future."

Wasn't that what sports were supposed to be all about?

Forget sports. Wasn't that what life was supposed to be all about? The ability to bounce back? The belief that better days were coming if we only believed enough, or worked hard enough? Tony C. taught me that.

So began the comebacks.

I followed each one, silently rooting for him, hoping he would get all the way back. Outside of the great year in 1970, when he hit 36 home runs, he never really did get back. Something had been lost that night in 1967 when he was hit in the face, something irretrievable.

One of the lessons sports teach is that life is not fair. I learned that watching what happened to Tony Conigliaro.

By this time my life had taken me far away from baseball. It was the early '70s. I rarely watched games, not even the Red Sox, didn't particularly care one way or the other. Conigliaro had been my last emotional link with it, and his career was over.

After that he became a sportscaster at Channel 10. I didn't enjoy watching him. He never seemed very good at it. He was there because of his name, not his ability. It was ironic. Here he was trying to get by on his name, when it had once been his ability that got him the name in the first place.

At one point during his stay in Providence I learned we had a mutual friend. I mentioned to this friend that in my younger years I had been a big fan of Conigliaro.

"Do you want to meet Tony?" my friend asked.

I never did. Already I had come to know that heroes always are better viewed from a distance. I also realized the strange bond I felt toward him existed in my own mind and nowhere else, and it was probably better to keep it there. There also was the sense back then that any emotional attachment I felt for him had happened long ago and far away, too far back in some fuzzy adolescence to be important anymore.

His heart attack in 1982 changed that. It left him in a wheelchair and in need of constant care, changing his life forever. It came as a personal shock to me. Weren't we the same age? Hadn't we, in a strange sense, both come to Boston on the same day in search of our futures? Why him?

Since then, I always flirted with the idea of going to see him and doing a story. I never did. Primarily because I knew that I didn't want to see him that way. As if to see him older, gray, a frail reminder of what he used to be, would have been too much like looking in the mirror of some personal future.

It's no fun to see your heroes grow old. Their demise as athletes are not only reminders that we are no longer young, but are signs of our own mortality. Tony Conigliaro taught me that, too. Sometimes the athletes we identify with most teach us things that have nothing to do with sports.

The eulogies have been wonderful, reminders of when he was one of the most feared hitters in baseball, one of the most charismatic athletes ever to play in Boston. There is talk of retiring his number so New England fans always will remember his baseball accomplishments.

But when I think of Tony C., what I remember the most is that spring afternoon in 1964. Back when we were both 19 years old and in Boston, in search of our futures, forever young.

Brother Adelard, courtesy of Mount Saint Charles Academy

"PERE DE HOCKEY" LEFT LEGACY IN R.I.

1990

"I don't miss anything because I have all these memories stored in my head."

—Brother Adelard

HARRISVILLE — One winter morning six years ago I drove to Harrisville in the northwest corner of the state, past pine trees and snow-covered fields, to see a man who had just turned 100 years old.

His name was Brother Adelard and he lived at the provincial house of the Brothers of the Sacred Heart, a tan building nestled under pine trees. His room was small, cluttered with memorabilia, only fitting for a man who had become known as the "pere de hockey."

It was a title he'd acquired long before, back in the early years of this century when he first introduced hockey to Rhode Island, skating with his students on a small pond in Central Falls. Back before the Bruins, and Mount St. Charles, before everything that had come to be associated with hockey around here.

So he sat there that morning, in the twilight of his years, and talked about how it used to be in the old days.

"Do you miss being so removed from the center of things now?" I asked.

"I don't miss anything," he said with a smile. "Because I have all these memories stored in my head."

That morning came rushing back at me yesterday when I read that Brother Adelard had died Sunday. He was 106. The story was on the obituary page. It said his real name was Brother Alphonse Beaudet, he had been born in Quebec, and first entered the Brothers of the Sacred Heart in 1904. It also said he was the father of schoolboy hockey in Rhode Island.

Stay in this business long enough, and you do a lot of stories. After a while many of them run together, blurring the memories. Only a few stand out. One of them, for me, was Brother Adelard. Maybe for no other reason except that by the time I first met him he already was 100, already had lived a couple of lifetimes.

But I like to think it was more than that.

I have never been a hockey fan. Not that I dislike it, mind you. It's just that I never paid much attention to it. I didn't play it as a kid. The National Hockey League was full of names I never heard of, victims of too much expansion and no national TV contract. Even the Bruins were unknown to me. By the time I became a sports writer seven years ago I could name you more players from the old Rhode Island Reds of my childhood than I could members of the Bruins.

I don't think I was all that unique.

The Orr era was long over in Boston. The Bruins were so faceless, most of them would have gone undetected in a lineup. There were virtually no hockey calls to the local sports talk shows. No one ever sat around the office and talked about the Bruins. In short, the Bruins often seemed to be little more than footnotes on the Boston scene.

But I could relate to the hockey Brother Adelard talked about that morning six years ago. It was all about frozen ponds, and small rinks. About cold feet, and makeshift uniforms. About early morning practices, and the sound of the puck ricocheting off the boards. For hockey is not a TV game. It's not a game for big arenas, where it's hard to see the puck. The soul of hockey is a frozen pond.

He had brought the sport down with him from his native Canada, a one-man pied piper for a game that already was a way of life where he came from, a game he once had learned on the frozen St. Lawrence River. He and his students cut down branches and used them for sticks. The goals were jackets held down with rocks. He played with his students. It was 1912.

A dozen years later he went to Woonsocket where a new school was opening, Mount St. Charles Academy. He became the school's treasurer. He also became the hockey coach.

It was the first great era of Mount St. Charles hockey. The old R.I Auditorium opened in 1926, became the showplace of Rhode Island schoolboy hockey. The Mount had its own outdoor rink, imported kids from Canada, who became known as the "Flying Frenchmen." For two years in the 1930's they were unofficial national champions. It's not for nothing that the Mount's rink is named after Brother Adelard.

Even after he stopped coaching in 1940, he never lost his love affair with the game. He skated into his 90's. Nor did he ever lose his love affair with Mount hockey.

Six years ago I asked him if he ever thought way back in 1912 that he one day would be known as "pere de hockey?"

"Not at all," he said. "It was just for the enjoyment of the boys." Then he had hesitated a beat, before adding quietly, "and for myself, too."

So when I saw the obit yesterday morning, I couldn't help but think of the timing of his death. For here we are in the middle of a hockey renaissance in New England, the re-birth of the Bruins, a resurgence of interest in the sport. Everywhere you go you hear people talking about the Bruins, watching the Bruins. No one can ignore them anymore, not even sports writers like myself who once tried to.

It said in the obit that, until he was 104, Brother Adelard was very active in fund raising for the order's African Missions, eventually giving it up because of failing eyesight. That was two years ago. So I like to think that Brother Adelard hung on just long enough to see hockey's resurgence around here. And that as the Bruins try and stay in contention for the Stanley Cup tonight, Brother Adelard is skating on some frozen pond somewhere, as timeless as a puck as it slides across the ice in an empty arena.

ALL-AMERICAN SWIMMER WRESTLES A DIFFERENT FOE

1990

"It had started out as a hobby and it had become my life."

—Kerry Donovan

NORTH KINGSTOWN – He was the Rhode Island schoolboy athlete of the year.

He set two national high school records in 200-meter swimming.

He went to Yale where he was a member of three relay teams that held world records.

He won an NCAA title in the 50-yard freestyle.

He was an All-American.

But one morning three years ago he sat in a trailer park in North Kingstown not caring whether he lived or died. He was hung over, feeling guilty because he had missed the bus that took him to work. He was 55 years old, and the promise of his youth seemed sacrificed on an altar of excess drinking, the drinking that had begun when his world had been a much simpler place.

"I took a bottle of pills," says Kerry Donovan with a wry smile. "But I must have taken the wrong kind. Because three hours later I woke up."

The drinking had started innocently enough. Social drinking at Yale. Vice president of one of the school's unofficial drinking societies. Boys will be boys. There were other swimmers who had sworn off drinking while they were in-season. Donovan never did.

"I wanted it all," he says. "I wanted swimming and I wanted parties. I was unwilling to make the choice. I thought I could do anything."

Looking back, he can see he always had a drinking problem. Not that he thought so at the time. So what if people were starting to tell him a decade later that he was drinking too much. Or that he lost a job on Wall Street because of it. Or that he went through a marriage and seemed to be bouncing from one investment job to another in New York City, trying to balance a career with a personal life that seemed to be getting more out of control.

Swimming had been Donovan's identity. It had made him special, set him apart. Now there was no more swimming.

"You try and make up for it in other ways," he says. "For me, I always had to be the big shot. I had to be a little wilder, a little crazier, had to drink more."

On this afternoon he is sitting in a doughnut shop in North Kingstown, near where he lives. His hair is all white now, but Donovan still moves with the easy grace of an athlete. He is 6-foot-1, long arms, wide shoulders, still with a swimmer's body after all the years.

In a few hours he will go to the Good Hope Center in West Greenwich, a residential treatment center for people with drug and alcohol problems. He's been a counselor there for three months. He says it's the best he's felt in recent memory. He has good relationships with his two children. He is sober. He hopes to have some influence on others, to help spare them some of the pain he's been through.

The swimming began when Donovan was 13. He joined the Wanskuck Boys Club in Providence's North End, working out twice a day. As a junior at La Salle in 1949, he broke a national high school record at a mete at Brown. The next year he did it again. It changed his life. It got him to a year at Phillips Exeter Academy in New Hampshire, light years away from the Manton Avenue of his childhood, then on to Yale, where the Ivy clings to the walls, the mood is old money, and the glee club sings about poor little lambs that have lost their way.

Yale was the No. 1 swimming school in the country then, its team's roster littered with future Olympians. The team swam in the Payne-Whitney Pool, one of sport's hallowed grounds. In Donovan's sophomore year, Yale won the national title.

But beneath all the success, there was the feeling he was different from most of the kids he saw around him, as if he still lived in two very different worlds, the Manton Avenue of his youth, and Ivy League Yale. He couldn't buy his clothes at Brooks Brothers as they could. He couldn't afford to go on weekend trips to New York. Sometimes he felt like someone peering through the window at the party at Yale. He was there because he was a great swimmer, not because he truly belonged there. He also had failed to make the Olympic team in 1952 in his freshman year, after thinking he was going to make it.

"It was the biggest disappointment of my life," he says. "I went into the shower room afterward and bawled my eyes out."

By the time he came back to Rhode Island it was 1972. He was 40 years old. He also was defeated.

"By this time I knew booze was the biggest thing in my life," he says, "but I was unwilling to do anything about it. It had started out as a hobby and it had become my life. It numbed the disappointment I had in myself."

He got a job as a security guard. For a while he worked third shift, which allowed him to go to a bar at seven in the morning and be able to tell himself that it was no big deal, because wasn't this his night? He became an expert at self-deception, at creating elaborate rationales for how his life had evolved. He told himself he liked being a security guard because it gave him time to read. He told himself that after years in corporate America, where someone is forever telling you what to do, he now controlled his own life. And alone in the middle of the night, that time when people tell themselves the truth, he told himself maybe the biggest lie of all, that he was hurting no one but himself.

"I was a fraud," he says. "I took perverse pleasure in doing the New York Times crossword puzzle in ink. I took pleasure knowing I was reading more books than anyone else. One of things drinking does is rob you of both your self-esteem and your ambition. I became unwilling to take any risks."

Through the years there had been several attempts to quit drinking. All failed. Until that morning three years ago when he woke up after taking a bottle of pills and realized "how pathetic I had become."

He can't remember when he was last in a pool, but there are times when he still has dreams about the races of his youth. And every once in a while, if he walks by a pool and smells the chlorine it all comes back to him. The endless workouts. The anxiety that lies in the pit of your stomach before a big race. The expectation. The exhilaration. The feeling of being 17 years old and knowing there's no way you can lose.

PHANTOM FRIAR SHOWS HIS SPIRIT

1991

"I've seen him doing all sorts of things for people that no one ever knows about."

—John Coughlin

PROVIDENCE — John Coughlin was in the first grade at St. Pius, a Catholic school in the Mt. Pleasant section of Providence, when he first met Duffy Dwyer.

It was long before Dwyer ever put on tights, a black cape and a helmet and ran around the Civic Center carrying a large Providence College flag, and transformed himself into "The Phantom Friar."

It was long before Dwyer ever won a national contest as "America's Nuttiest Sports Nut." It was long before he ever started doing local sports talk shows, something he's done on WALE and WICE the past few years.

And it was long before Dwyer ever got cancer, which has now cost him his kidney and may end up costing him his life, an illness he first learned he had last December.

"Duffy's always been a very special person," says Coughlin, now a Providence policeman, "someone who's concerned about people. A lot of people know him from running around the Civic Center, but I know him from putting on a Santa Claus outfit and visiting everyone's nieces and nephews. I've seen him reading to kids. I've seen him doing all sorts of things for people that no one ever knows about."

Dwyer is also one of those people who is impossible not to like,

The Phantom Friar, courtesy of Providence College

a big, warm-hearted man with the special ability to make everyone around him feel a little better.

But it was "The Phantom Friar" that first gave him his public identity, and it happened quite by accident. It was the Big East Tournament in Madison Square Garden in 1986 and, as the story goes, some of Duffy's friends wanted to get their faces on television and figured that if Duffy dressed up in some weird outfit and stood by the court they might sneak into the picture.

So he put on the tights, a black cape, striped shorts and a helmet - what he called his combination Darth Vader "Captain Chaos" outfit - and became an unofficial PC mascot. Combine that with the fact that Dwyer weighed over 300 pounds at the time and we're talking about a sight that people didn't soon forget.

The birth of "The Phantom Friar."

Originally, it was only supposed to be a one-game thing, but the next week he brought the routine into the Civic Center for the NIT. It was Rick Pitino's first year as coach, excitement was starting to build, and "The Phantom Friar" became part of the atmosphere. In an age where everything seems choreographed in college basketball and halftime shows often look as glitzy as Vegas floor shows, there was something wonderfully goofy and spontaneous about this bearded man in tights and a cape running around the Civic Center.

He did it for five seasons, before giving it up because he began fearing his presence was taking away from the cheerleaders. He then started being a sports broadcaster. He created his own Dwyer Sports Network, started appearing on local talk shows, a fan with a microphone, a big-hearted man who wants all the home teams to do well.

Then one night in December at a PC game he discovered blood in his urine and everything got more complicated. He had a CAT-scan in February. In March he had a kidney removed. Now the cancer has spread to his chest and his groin.

Yet he has remained upbeat, positive, the way he always was

when the Friars were losing and time was running out and "The Phantom Friar" would run around the Civic Center still believing that if everyone just rooted hard enough everything would turn out all right in the end. He still goes to work for the Department of Transportation when he feels good enough. He just started again on the radio. He is trying to live as normal a life as he can, amidst the treatments and the uncertainty. The worst case scenario is that he could be dead in two years.

"The word cancer strikes fear," Dwyer says. "People see it as a death sentence. But there are a lot of people who beat it. I have days when I'm fatigued, and there are some times riding in the car or something when my mind will wander and I'll say 'I'm dying' - but then I realize we all are. I can't believe this is going to stop me. I have to believe that the right medicine and a little help from the Almighty and things will turn out all right. It's like with PC. I always thought they could come back, and I think I can, too."

Still, these are not the best of times for Duffy Dwyer. He is 36 years old and he's in a fight more urgent than whether the Friars can come back against Villanova. There are medicines to take, bills to pay. Duffy likes to say that after all the games and all the gyms the big game has now come down to him against cancer. One-on-one.

So come Saturday night, Coughlin and some of Dwyers' childhood friends, along with Channel 6 sportscaster Ken Bell, are running an appreciation night for Dwyer in the Peterson Recreation Center on the PC campus. It's an event designed to help him with his soaring medical expenses. It's also a public thank you for all the times Duffy Dwyer made everyone else feel a little better, if only for a moment in the Civic Center. Ironically, it's just the kind of event that in better times Dwyer would be running for someone else.

"All those people he got to stand up in the Civic Center and rally around PC?" said Coughlin. "Now it's time for these people to rally around him."

ABDUL ABDULLAH RETURNING HOME

1992

"I've come too far to quit now."

—ABDUL ABDULLAH

PROVIDENCE — He got the call a few weeks ago from his friend Jamie Benton, the former Boston College player who works at the South Side Boys Club in South Providence.

"Coach Fran called and asked about you," Benton said.

"Who?" he asked.

He was told "Coach Fran" was Providence College assistant coach Fran Fraschilla.

"What's he want?" he asked.

"He wants you, Ab," Benton said.

Three thousand miles away, in a trailer in Los Angeles, he couldn't believe what he was hearing. Abdul Abdullah, the former Community College of Rhode Island star who grew up in the streets of Providence and once lived within sight of the Civic Center, was hearing that his life was about to significantly change.

For the past few months, he'd been living several blocks from the L.A.'s storied Forum, going to Compton Junior College about 10 miles away. Essentially, he'd been in basketball exile, in a California junior college with the vague promise that if all went well academically he might end up next year at Arizona State.

The best point guard to come out of Rhode Island since Ernie DiGregorio two decades ago, all dressed up with no place to play.

This past December, after visiting Providence during semester break, he took a bus for three days to get back to California. He calls it the worst three days of his life, alone on a bus in the middle of nowhere, facing an uncertain future, far from home.

"What kept you from turning back?" he was asked.

"The dream is what motivates me every day," he said yesterday over the phone.

The dream is to play big-time college basketball, and when I first met Abdullah that dream might have been located on the dark side of the moon as far as he was concerned. It was three years ago. He was a senior at Central High School at the time. He was ineligible to play basketball. He was not going to graduate. He appeared about ready to become just another lost inner-city kid whose dreams had turned to dust, another victim of a neighborhood that all too often eats its young.

His father had died when he was just a kid. His mother had left a couple of years earlier to go back to New York, essentially leaving Abdul and his older brother to fend for themselves. On the day I talked with him, he seemed lost, overwhelmed, defeated. But since then, he has gotten his GED degree, gone to CCRI for two years, and spent this year at two junior colleges in California. Somehow, he has survived. Over the weekend, he signed a national letter of intent to attend Providence College in the fall. It's based on Abdullah successfully completing his current classes at Compton and probably taking two summer classes.

That dream of his is real close.

"It's unbelievable," he said. "It came as a complete surprise. This year has been a lot of anxiety for me. But being away cleared my head totally. Being away was the key to making the decision to come home. When I first left, I thought I never wanted to go back home again. But now I know I do. I did what I had to do, and now I'm ready to come back."

PC's recruiting of Abdullah began a couple of months ago. PC coach Rick Barnes felt he needed a point guard to be able to come in and play right away. He also has come to know that PC "isn't

Duke, isn't Notre Dame. For us to be successful we have to take some 'high risk' kids," Barnes said. He knew of Abdullah's ability from having seen him play two years ago when PC was recruiting Ken McDonald out of CCRI. He talked to Benton. He talked to McDonald. He talked to people who knew Abdullah.

"If we were going to recruit him, I wanted to know everything about him," Barnes said. "If we were going to take an academic risk, he was going to have to be a good person."

Two weeks ago, Barnes went to California to see him, spent two days there.

"I got in his face," Barnes said. "I told him what to expect if he came here. That our players are going to be good people. They are going to go to class. And they are going to work hard."

Barnes also knows the perceptions that surround Abdullah. That he's an academic disaster. That drug rumors once swirled around him, back when he was at Central and his high school career was unraveling. That ghetto stars often burn out quickly, and Abdullah has spent much of his career as a ghetto star, seemingly a prisoner of the environment that created him.

"I don't worry about public perception," Barnes said, "because people don't know. If you saw where he's living you wouldn't believe it. To just survive there is an achievement."

He was sitting in the cafeteria in the basement of Alumni Hall, and at one point, Franklin Western, a PC player, walked by.

"He just became a better player," Barnes said with a sly smile, referring to Abdullah's recruitment, "and he doesn't even know it."

For Barnes knows Abdullah has the ability to jump start the P.C.'s offense. Knows he has the flair to light up the Civic Center. Knows that it's never been a question about Abdullah's ability, merely the baggage that comes with him. Eventually, the talk turned to whether Abdullah will be able to succeed in the structured environment the PC players live in. Barnes began talking about how once upon a time he grew up poor in North Carolina, about how once upon a time some people gave him chances when maybe they didn't have a lot of reasons to. And how that ultimately changed his life.

"I know that you can't quit on people until they've quit on themselves," he said, "and Abdul's never quit on himself. Even in situations when a lot of people would have."

And sure, Barnes wants Abdullah because he thinks Abdullah can be the point guard the Friars need. Certainly, the school would not be taking a chance on him if he weren't a basketball player. We're not talking purely selfless reasons here. We're talking about the pragmatics of big-time college basketball. Yet Barnes also feels he can change Abdullah's life.

"I told him I can't guarantee that he'll graduate. I can't guarantee how much playing time he's going to get. All I can guarantee is an opportunity to change his life. An opportunity for him to make choices in his life. That's all I'm doing is giving him the vehicle. He has to drive it. I told him that if one day he ends up back where he is now, it will be his choice."

Abdullah says he understands.

"I've come too far to quit now," he said.

Abdul Abdullah, the best point guard to come out of Rhode Island in two decades, is coming home.

ROGER CLEMENS, ANTHONY MANZO AND CHICKENS!

1993

"Gladys, Gladys, wake up."

—ANTHONY MANZO

NORTH PROVIDENCE — The idea kind of snuck up on him.

He was lying in bed one night, his wife asleep beside him, but he wasn't counting sheep. No, he was counting chickens. Wood-roasted chickens. The kind that cook in a big oven he had seen in Montreal.

He had been flirting with the idea of opening a restaurant for a while, he and his brother Jeffrey. After all, their father owned one in North Providence for years, and they had grown up in the business.

But what kind of restaurant? Now, in the middle of the night, it came to him. A fast-food chicken restaurant. One named after a sports star, a name big enough to lure people through the door. One that could be franchised all over New England. He closed his eyes and saw chickens instead of sheep. Then he began to shake his wife.

"Gladys, Gladys, wake up," he said, the words tumbling over themselves. "I got it. I'm going to open up a restaurant."

"Yeah, yeah, yeah," she said, half-asleep. "Go to sleep."

But there was no stopping him now. He liked nothing better than a new idea, and this one promised to be even better than becoming one of the "Blues Brothers," the schtick he and his brother-in-law, Joe Mac, had been doing at the Civic Center the last seven years at Providence College basketball games.

"And here's the topper," he said to her. "We're going to name it after Roger Clemens."

Who better than the Rocket? Larry Bird? Too old. Ray Bourque? Mike Greenwell? He tossed these around in his mind like biscuits in a box of take-out chicken. But he knew it had to be the Rocket, New England's numero uno sports superstar.

"But you don't know Roger Clemens," his wife said, turning over.

"I don't now," he said, "but I will."

The next day he bounced the idea off his brother, who also is partner with him in Anthony's Jewelers in North Providence and East Greenwich. He already could picture the restaurant in his mind. Roger Clemens' Sports World, with other ones coming later, sold as franchises.

"You're a nut," his brother told him. "And if you did any drinking last night, get off the booze."

"Wait and see," he replied.

So it began for Anthony Manzo.

It was September of 1990.

Seems that Manzo already knew Red Sox infielder Marty Barrett, who once had bought a diamond at Anthony's Jewelers. Manzo asked Barrett to ask Clemens if he might be interested in putting his name on a new restaurant. Clemens was. So Barrett arranged a meeting on New Year's Eve in Las Vegas where Clemens was going to be visiting. Manzo and his brother rented a suite, were all set to give Clemens the big presentation. But Clemens was about an hour late and Manzo thought he was being stiffed.

"Jeffrey and I were sweating from our temples," Manzo said.

The two of them had their wives on lookout in the lobby, waiting to spot Clemens. Soon, the phone rang in the suite. There had been a Clemens sighting in the hotel.

"He and Marty and some guy in sunglasses came in and I started to explain 'Sports World,' " Manzo says, "but it was like no one was listening. Roger wasn't even looking at me. I was getting all choked up. Then I said to myself, 'You haven't choked at anything yet,' and I started rolling."

The meeting got better after that. Clemens admitted he'd been giving Manzo a hard time. The guy in the sunglasses turned out to be former Sox pitcher Al Nipper. Clemens finally told Manzo to keep going with the project.

The next night the group went to Caesar's Palace, first row. They were there to see Little Richard. Before Little Richard came on, Manzo went on stage and took the microphone. Manzo's not exactly shy. Soon he had one half of the audience yelling "Little," the other half yelling "Richard," all with his inimitable style that once had the "Blues Brothers" revving up the Civic Center.

Clemens was hooked and a friendship began.

Now it's roughly two and a half years later and Roger Clemens Sports World is set to open Friday on Bald Hill Road in the Douglas Drug Plaza. There is a large, green-and-white awning out front. Move over Colonel Sanders, and tell Frank Perdue the news.

So there was Manzo and his brother yesterday noon at his creation. They were sitting in a teal booth, ("The color of the '90's," Manzo says,) and the walls were dominated by four, large, action drawings of Clemens in various stages of his windup. Behind him was the Roger Clemens memorabilia center. To his left was the Roger Clemens souvenir counter. On the table in front of him was the menu, one that says wood-roasted chicken is low in calories, fat and cholesterol, all done in a baseball motif. Call it a living memorial to the Rocket.

And you thought only Wade Boggs liked chicken?

Clemens hasn't seen any of this yet. He is due to take a look sometime next week. No matter. Manzo peers into the future and sees endless Roger Clemens' Sports World restaurants, from sea to shining sea. He sees himself and Roger in business together forever, the best pitcher in baseball and a guy from North Providence who had a vision.

"Do you believe it?" he says. "All this started from lying around in bed with a dream. This is a local dream come true."

With a bucket of chicken to go.

HOOP STAR BATTLES MS

1992

"It bothers me that I can no longer play, but I'll do what I can do."

—Mike Hazard

SMITHFIELD — It was two years ago when Mike Hazard first heard the news that has changed his life.

He had problems with his hearing, then his vision. Every time he tried to play basketball, he got dizzy. So he went to a doctor, and there were tests and more tests, and now the doctor was telling him he had multiple sclerosis.

Mike Hazard, one of the greatest schoolboy basketball players to come out of Rhode Island in the past two decades, was being told that his life had significantly changed.

"I didn't know what to think," he says. "But I wasn't really scared because I could still do all the things I wanted to do. I could still go out and fool around playing basketball. Now . . . "

His voice seems to trail off.

We are sitting in the kitchen of his house that adjoins Esmond Village, an apartment complex where he does the maintenance. A few minutes earlier, he and his five-year-old son Jamaal had walked across the small stretch of grass that leads to his side door. He had limped noticeably, his left leg all but dragging behind him.

"I've had trouble with it for the past six months," he says, "but the past couple of months you can really notice it."

Jamaal is in the next room watching television. Hazard's 10-year-old daughter Lashawanna is at school. Hazard talks about what he knows about MS, how it's an unpredictable disease. How it can get worse, get better, go into remission for years. How no one knows what it will do.

"What worries me is that someday I won't be able to do things with them," he says. "Those are the things I think about now."

It is all very complicated, of course.

Then again, Hazard's world never has been easy.

In a sense, Mike Hazard always will belong to a certain era in Rhode Island sports. In the mid-'70s, he was one of four kids who made up what might have been the best high school basketball team ever in Rhode Island. Willie Washington. Dobie Dennis. Billy Perry. Mike Hazard. As if their public lives had become intertwined, a basketball foursome, even though the reality was that, individually, they were very different.

They also were part of a tradition, the end of an era that saw Central High School win seven straight state titles, the inner-city school dominating the inner-city game. Hazard was the shooter, the 6-foot-4 forward who played without expression. Soul on ice. He was the quiet one, the one who didn't hang out on the street. The others called him the All-American boy.

Yet, beneath the high school acclaim, he also carried the baggage of the inner-city with him.

He had grown up in the Chad Brown project in Providence's North End, shy, withdrawn, locked in a private world. He had no interest in school, no real interest in anything. He was one of four children raised by his mother Doris. His father lived in Providence, but had little to do with him. It left emotional scars he didn't even know he had until many years later.

"I play with my kids," he says. "I take them places. I watch them grow and do amazing things and I think about how my father missed all that."

For years he wanted to confront his father. Wanted to ask him why. Why had he left? Why had he chosen not to be a part of his children's lives? Why? But he never did. Then one day his father died, and it was too late.

"But I'll never do to my kids what my father did to me," he says.

In many ways, basketball saved Hazard, gave him an identity when he so desperately needed one.

"I don't know what would have happened to me without it," he says.

But when the cheers at Central ended, he had little clue about his future. At the beginning of his senior year, letters had started arriving from colleges. He put them in a box in his room. They are still there today.

"I had no idea of the process," he once said. "I was waiting for someone to take hold of me."

He ended up at Northeastern. Also there to play basketball was Billy Lynch, whose father was the mayor of Pawtucket at the time. The two became roommates. The white kid whose father was one of the most recognizable political figures in the state; the black kid from Chad Brown.

"You couldn't get him to talk back then," Lynch once said. "He was so quiet he wouldn't say two words."

The next year, he went to CCRI, which had become a Warwick version of Central. Washington, Dennis and Perry were there. Hazard made it an old, familiar foursome. He wanted to go to Providence College and play in the Civic Center, the brass ring that dangles in front of so many local kids, just out of reach. The school strung him along that summer, but in late August, still not sure about PC, nervous about the future, he went to Acadia University in Novia Scotia. That first year, he came back to play against a good URI team. He scored 27 points. If there ever were any doubts Mike Hazard could play major college basketball, they were erased that night.

He played in Acadia for three years; left without a degree.

When I did a story on him seven years ago, he had heard for

years that he could have played at PC, or URI, could have played somewhere more in the public eye than Acadia. But there were no regrets. He had liked Canada, had even thought of staying there. He already had gone to work for the Lynches then, working on the apartment complex that the Lynch family manages. He was living next door, in a suburban setting that is far away from the Providence of his youth. He was still playing basketball in various local leagues, still proving to anyone who saw him that very few players came out of Rhode Island in the past couple of decades any better than Mike Hazard.

He played in a Pawtucket summer league with Billy Lynch and his brothers. He was the first black in the league. He played in the North Providence summer league, again on Lynch's team. More and more, it seemed as if he were putting his past behind him. Now, he hardly ever sees the guys he once played high school basketball with, the ones he once was so linked with.

"The only time I go to Providence now is to see my mother," he says.

Hazard was an assistant coach at St. Raphael Academy in Pawtucket for four years, spent the past winter refereeing jayvee and girl's games. Now he wants to start coaching youth teams. If he can no longer play basketball, he will coach it, as though the game is too imbedded in him to just put it away someplace.

"It bothers me that I can no longer play," he says, "but I'll do what I can do."

He has more doctors to see, more tests to take. One doctor thinks his leg problem might be the result of a disk problem in his neck. Another thinks it's a direct result of his MS. Who knows? When he gets depressed, he thinks of his sister Charleen, who has sickle cell anemia and is in a wheelchair.

"My sister is in worse shape than I am," he says, "and that's one of the things that keeps me going. I look at her and I can't feel sorry for myself. And there's no sense getting down about it, because that can make the disease worse. So I try to look forward now."

Jamaal comes into the kitchen, pushing a truck, as I get ready to leave. Mike Hazard takes his hand and they go outside into the sunshine. Mike limps into the side-yard. Jamaal looks up at him and smiles.

LOPES FINALLY GETTING A BIT OF HIS DUE

1993

"If you were from the right side of the tracks you became a celebrity. If you weren't, you were ignored."

—Davey Lopes

PROVIDENCE — Shortly after 2:30 yesterday afternoon, Rhode Island's most unappreciated sports hero walked into the lobby of the Days Hotel.

He soon was to be given the Rhode Island NAACP chapter's distinguished service award at its annual dinner in Seekonk, Mass. The obvious question: Was he flattered?

"Very much so," said Davey Lopes. "Especially because it's here. I don't expect anything from here, so when it comes it's a shock."

Here.

Home.

A strong case can be made that Lopes is our most unappreciated local sports star. How many other Rhode Island kids can you name who played in four World Series, led the National League in stolen bases two straight years? How many Rhode Island kids who grow up to be successful pro athletes could walk through the Warwick Mall unnoticed?

Lopes always has been aware of his lack of celebrity here. In the summer of 1988, back when he was a coach for the Texas Rangers, he said one night in Fenway Park that people in Providence probably didn't even know he had been in the big leagues.

"Why?" he was asked.

"Why?" he asked. "Because I was from the wrong side of the tracks. If you were from the right side of the tracks you became a celebrity. If you weren't, you were ignored. That's just the way it was. It was black and white."

He paused a beat.

"Literally."

He didn't sound bitter that night. He didn't sound angry. If the words had an edge to them, his tone didn't. As if this were a battle he'd lost a long time ago. As if this was just the way it was and he had learned a long time ago that there was nothing he was going to do to change it.

The irony is he's as Rhode Island as a coffee cabinet.

He grew up in East Providence. He played in the Fox Point Little League. He moved to South Providence when he was 10, came of age playing in numerous youth leagues in the city. He went to La Salle. He played baseball in the Amateur League.

Adding to the irony was that he was a great story, too. He was never some baseball prodigy, some kid for whom the major leagues was virtually a given. He had gone to two small colleges in the Midwest, two places that don't send players to major-league baseball. He wasn't even drafted until he was 21, and even that came in the 28th round.

He was a kid from South Providence, one of 10 kids in a home without a father, chasing a baseball dream.

"The first time I ran out on the field in Dodger Stadium, I had tears in my eyes," he said yesterday. "Icouldn't believe it. Davey Lopes from Providence, Rhode Island."

He's now in his second year as a coach for the Baltimore Orioles. The carrot that dangles in front of him is a managerial job, but he's been around the game long enough to know that so much of who gets job and who doesn't is politics, and says that he will not be hurt if he never gets a chance to manage. One senses that the key is staying in the game, the only thing he ever wanted, the dream that started back in what now sometimes must seem like a different life.

"Do you think people around here have ever understood how difficult it was to make it considering where you came from?" he was asked.

"No," he said. "They have no idea. None. I probably had a better chance of winning the lottery."

He went on to have a career out of some personal fantasy. Fifteen years in the major leagues. World Series. All-Star teams. Recognition. A world so different from the South Providence sandlots of his youth.

But, strangely enough, about the only place where he didn't get recognition was his hometown. Here. No matter that he always had a lot of extended family here, roots that run deep. Or that he always was here for a while in the offseason. In a state where we usually grab our sports heroes to our hearts and never let them go, Davey Lopes always seemed the forgotten stepchild.

"l never really could understand it," he said. "It's not like this was an area that sent a lot of players to the major leagues. And I wouldn't be honest if I said it didn't bother me. It wasn't like I was a druggie or anything, or got in trouble."

He paused a bit.

"That was the most disturbing thing. But it was something I couldn't control and I learned to accept it."

So it's been nice that there are signs that this benign neglect is changing. Rhode Island's most unappreciated sports hero is starting to be appreciated. A few years ago, he was inducted into the R. l. Heritage Hall of Fame. In November of '91, the South Providence Recreation Center, the building where he spent so many of his childhood hours, was renamed in his honor. Last night it was the award from the NAACP.

"It's been great," he said. "1 think the attention means more when it happens in your hometown."

"So this is still your home?" he was asked.

Davey Lopes look surprised.

"1 never had any doubts about it," he said. "People around here might have had doubts about it. But I didn't. This has always been home."

The only difference is now his home is beginning to recognize it, too.

Courtesy of Boston Sports Museum

BOSTON GARDEN MEMORIES

1995

BOSTON — It was every building out of your childhood. Every old gym where the locker room was too small, and there weren't enough showers, and you had to hang some of your clothes on nails. Every old gym where the stairs wore the remnants of decades of scuffling feet, where there were dead spots on the court, and where there was always a stage at one end.

The Boston Garden.

It might have been the place where both the Celtics and Bruins played. It might have been in Boston. It might have been big. It might have had all those banners hanging from the rafters, a tradition that you could almost reach out and touch.

But its soul was every building out of your childhood.

There's no overestimating the significance of the Garden to anyone who grew up in New England before the '70s, for the simple reason that the Garden was all there was. There was no Providence Civic Center, with its good sightlines and modern sound system. No Hartford Civic Center. No Worcester Centrum. No civic arenas in New Haven or Springfield.

Just the Garden.

With its obstructed seats, smoke that hung over the court like summer haze. With its long hallways that led you out of the lobby of North Station like some maze. With its funny-looking floor. With the seats that were too small, and the rows that were too cramped, and the organ music that always seemed stuck on some '50s song sheet. A building that looked as if it came out of some old movie about the Depression, the grit and the grime all but burnished into everything, right there underneath the elevated train tracks.

The Garden.

It became the antithesis of the Forum in L.A., just as the Celtics became the antithesis of the Lakers. Those two teams were the perfect alter-egos back then. The Lakers, with their flash and their showtime and the movie stars who sat in the front row of the Forum. The Celtics, with their work ethic and their banners in the rafters and the smell of a thousand of Red's old cigars, all but a part of the dirty Garden walls.

Always the Garden.

In a sense that was the Garden's last great hurrah, the Celtics of the Bird Era. That was when you just knew the Celtics were not going to lose a big game in the Garden. Just knew that something would happen to the opposing team. Just knew that somehow the old leprechaun would come out of the murky past and sit on the basket and swat away enemy shots.

That feeling's been gone for a while now. The past few years the Garden has just seemed old, a dowager who can't hide the years no matter how much makeup she uses. It had become more difficult to come into the Garden and see the romance. Now you just saw the years. There were just too many of them.

So the Garden is ready for the wrecker's ball.

But the memories will remain, a thousand snapshots of Boston sports history. Like the memories of childhood.

And of every old gym you ever knew.

A DRIVEWAY, A SANCTUARY AND A SENSE OF SELF

1995

"Would I have been different without basketball?"

—Bill Reynolds

BARRINGTON — It's just a driveway.

It's at the end of a backyard, in front of a tan garage, and yesterday it was covered with a coating of snow as I sat across the street in my parked car and stared at it.

So why was it so important? Why had this been, in so many ways, my spiritual center?

The years came rushing back in a montage of images, a personal newsreel going back to the tail end of the sleepy Eisenhower '50s, back when Barrington was making the transformation from small town to suburb. In a sense, Barrington and I had grown up together. It's conjecture who turned out better.

I saw myself as I had been then, an adolescent in the driveway, shooting baskets alone, dreaming my dreams, lost in some solitary world. On snowy days, I shoveled off the driveway. On cold January days, I'd shoot with a glove on my left hand, leaving my right free to grip the frozen ball. Nights, I'd take a flashlight and lay it on the ground so it angled up on the basket, a beacon in the darkness.

Day after day. Night after night. Playing imaginary games in my head. The sound of the ball slapping against the pavement, echoing through the stillness. This sanctuary from homework, from family tensions, from the pressures of adolescence.

Courtesy of Brown University

Basketball had become an obsession, quite simply. It had determined who my friends were. It would later determine where I went to school, and what I studied once I got there. More importantly, basketball had given me a sense of self at a time when I had desperately needed one.

It was only later that I would come to resent it, and see how one-dimensional it had been. By then I was a senior in college. Vietnam had complicated everything for my generation, had made me start to question things I never had questioned before. And why didn't I know anything about literature? About art? About serious music? Why didn't I know anything about anything other than whether my jump shot went in or not?

If I had spent all that time practicing the piano I'd be in the concert halls of Europe now - at least, that's what I liked to tell people. Instead, I had spent my time shooting baskets on this driveway, refining a skill that was to lose its real importance by the time I was only 22.

Now, on this foggy afternoon so many years later, I am not quite sure what it had all been about. Off to the right was the house I had grown up in. I hadn't been inside in 27 years. I don't know who lives there now. I don't know anyone who lives in the neighborhood now. The houses are the same; the people are not. But then, nothing stays the same.

To the left of the driveway was a backboard with a hoop, not like the one that had been attached to the garage when I was a kid. Does that mean there's some other kid in this house? A kid who comes out here alone and shoots baskets in the dark? And does he have the same dreams?

I kept staring at the snow-covered driveway.

Just a driveway.

It was much smaller than I remembered. The driveway. The houses around it. The entire neighborhood. My world once; now just memories. I know that in some tangible way the hours I spent out here served me well. They got me a sliver of high school fame. They got me into a college I never would have been able to get into without basketball. Now I make a living writing about sports, and most of the time I consider myself very fortunate to be able to do so.

Yet I know I have paid a price, too.

I know that my childhood obsession defined me, narrowed my options early, shaped my view of the world. Would I have been different without basketball? No doubt. Would my life have been better? Who can tell? I think about this often, about how capricious it all is sometimes, the way some early choice can determine so much of what happens later. We often pay for our obsessions, in one way or another.

Nothing, after all, is ever quite what it seems, whether it's a dream, a life, or a snow-covered driveway in a quiet neighborhood on a foggy January afternoon. Even now, I wished I could go out on the court and fire up a few jumpers in the cold.

Just for old times' sake.

HERREN'S WOES CREATE HEAVY HEART

1997

"Tomorrow will be a better day."

—Chris Herren

PROVIDENCE — When Celtics draft choice Len Bias died of a drug overdose a decade ago, Larry Bird said it was one of the saddest things he'd ever heard. So it was with me Tuesday night upon hearing that Fall River's Chris Herren had left the Fresno State basketball team to deal with a substance-abuse problem, saying he needed some time to get his life "back in order."

"It's like something got to me the past few weeks," Herren said to me over the phone late Tuesday night. "And if I didn't get a grip on it, I knew I was going down bad."

And it's more than the fact that Herren was the centerpiece of a book I once wrote called Fall River Dreams, which chronicled his junior year at Durfee High School, back when it was apparent that his basketball ability could take him far away from the small high school gyms of southeastern Massachusetts; back when I spent countless hours with him. Or that I have watched him come of age, change from a 17-year-old who didn't even have a driver's license into the leading scorer on the 12th-ranked college basketball team in the country.

It is, quite simply, that Chris Herren always carries a large piece of my heart with him.

Maybe that's because beneath all the ability and all the fame, all the outward trappings that are supposed to mean everything but often don't, there's always been a certain fragility to Herren.

He's always been a kid struggling with his own demons; a private struggle that all too often got played out in public, as if all the cheers and attention carried a steep price tag. There's always been a certain vulnerability to him, beneath all the toughness and street grit, the public persona.

Basketball always has been the easy part.

Tuesday night's news reaffirmed that.

"This is a winnable battle, and I had been winning," he told reporters in Fresno of his battle with substance abuse, the words coming through tears. "But I am here today to tell everyone that I have had a setback. That I have slipped up."

Ironically, it came just three days after he had been the star of Fresno State's nationally televised win over UMass, a game in which he'd scored 19 points and been interviewed by ESPN's Digger Phelps. A time when Herren seemed at the top of the world he had worked so hard to create for himself the last few years, ever since leaving Boston College and going across the country to California to rebuild both a life and a basketball career.

He had done that, a wonderful redemption story. And it all seemed a long way from the Fall River of his youth.

He had gone to coach Jerry Tarkanian, the savior of lost basketball souls, and changed his hoop life. He had gotten in shape. Had stopped drinking. Had been the MVP of a Fresno State team that went to the NIT last year, even though he hadn't played the previous two years. More importantly, he had changed his lifestyle. No more late nights. No more self-destructive behavior. The realization that life had become more complicated than taking the ball to the basket against Somerset. The realization that an athletic career is fragile, can blow up in your face for reasons that have nothing to do with what happens on a basketball court.

"I can't do those things and do what I'm trying to do," he said a year ago. "Maybe some people can. But I can't. I know that now. I just can't do those things and be successful."

But dealing with substance abuse is a daily battle, a work-in-progress. There are no complete victories, no happy endings with bows on them. It's an everyday grind, one day at a time, even for basketball stars who live their lives in the middle of cheers. And it's a far more dangerous opponent than anyone Chris Herren plays against on the court.

Tuesday night's announcement reinforced that.

"How are you doing?" I asked.

"I feel relieved right now," he said. "That I don't have to hide anymore."

He was only a couple hours removed from his press conference. It took courage to stand up there and say he'd messed up, and I told him that. Took courage to admit he needs help, that this is a difficult time in his life and that he needs support if he's going to get through it. That going public with his problem was the first step, a dramatic gesture that hopefully will be the springboard for him to once again take control of his life.

Yesterday, he entered a treatment program in Fresno. The plan is for him to rejoin the basketball team if he successfully completes the program. The time frame is three weeks, maybe less.

"I know I can do it," he said. "I have to do it."

But the stakes are higher now. He is a glamour player on one of the country's glamour college basketball teams, a player with pro potential. His press conference was carried live by the Fresno television stations. It was carried on ESPN's SportsCenter, a national story. Unlike three years ago, when he was a freshman at Boston College, his private struggle has become very public.

"I can't worry about that," he said. "I have to get myself straightened out and come to grips with this. If I don't deal with this, then the basketball isn't going to be any good for me, anyway."

He hesitated on the phone.

"You going to be all right?" I asked.

"This was the worst day," said Herren. "Having to tell my mother and father. The press conference. Having to face the media. Having everyone know. Tomorrow will be a better day."

POSTSCRIPT: Since leaving basketball and achieving long-term sobriety, Chris Herren has devoted his life to helping others overcome their substance abuse problems. In 2011, he founded a national non-profit organization, the Herren Project, which offers an array of treatment options and avenues of support for the struggling addict.

2000-2010

JAMES QUINN, 94, NATION'S OLDEST LIVING MEDAL WINNER

2000

"I had my time."

—JAMES QUINN

CRANSTON — It seems a long way from Sydney and these 2000 Olympic Games.

No TV lights. No cheering crowds. No Bob Costas. None of the things that have become as much a part of the Olympics as medal counts and national anthems. Instead, just Dean Estates, a quiet neighborhood in Cranston.

But there's a piece of Olympic history here in this small white house, here with this 94-year-old man who is this country's oldest living gold-medal winner. His name is James Quinn, and 72 years ago he ran into his sliver of sports immortality. On this afternoon he sits in his living room with his wife, Katherine. He's sitting here with his Olympic memories of a different time, a different place.

"The Olympics then were a country fair compared to what they are today," he says. "The stadium was like something you might see Cranston East play in."

It was held in Amsterdam in July of 1928. The IX Olympiad.

Quinn was 21 that long- ago summer. He had just graduated from Holy Cross, and he had qualified for the Olympic team by winning the 100-yard dash in the prestigious IC4A's at Harvard Stadium, running 9.9 on a muddy track.

So by the time he got to Amsterdam he already was an incredible success story, a skinny kid who had grown up in Brooklyn and had arrived unnoticed at Holy Cross. He hadn't been recruited. He hadn't been some teenage prodigy, defined by his sport. He wasn't someone who had grown up dreaming of sports glory. He didn't even get any scholarship money until his senior year. He was just a kid who liked to run, someone whose natural speed would take him places he never thought he could get to.

"Did you have anyone sponsoring you?" he is asked.

"Are you kidding?" he says. "The answer is no."

Actually, he did get $25 from the New York Athletic Club. And one day a tailor from New York came to Worcester to measure him for some suits. That was about it.

In Amsterdam, on that July day, he ran the second leg of the winning 400-meter relay what turned out to be the fastest leg beating Germany and Great Britain. He won a gold medal. An Olympic gold medal.

Then it ended.

Just like that.

So what did Quinn do then? Did he come back and start training for the '32 Olympics? Did he come home and try to take that gold medal into the marketplace and see how much it would bring? Did he try and live off it?

"I quit," he says simply. "It was time to move on."

Think about that for a second.

The Olympics are so much about marketing now, as if sports fame is something to be bartered, just another bargaining chip in the larger game of commerce. Bruce Jenner parlayed winning the decathlon in the '76 Olympics into a national name and a lucrative endorsement career that exists to this day. Mary Lou Retton parlayed her Olympic gold into a career as a motivational speaker. Virtually everyone comes home and tries to cash in, gold medal as calling card to celebrity and a life in the spotlight.

Quinn just came home to start the next chapter in his life. To get on with things. Being a sprinter was like something he used to love, ultimately stowed away in some childhood footlocker, along with the old trophies and the memories.

"I had to start making some money," he says.

He didn't even attend the parade that New York mayor Jimmy Walker held for the Olympians. Instead, he went to work in his family's small jewelry company in New York. But then came the Depression and times got tough. Eventually, he got a sales job with the jewelry company Dieges & Clust in Providence, moving to Rhode Island in the late '50s. He's been here ever since.

"Did you ever miss running?" he is asked.

"No," he says.

Maybe it's not surprising.

Back then, being an Olympic athlete wasn't a full-time job. There was no Olympic training center in Colorado Springs. No sponsors. No appearance money. No money, period. In Quinn's era, the Olympics were still what they originally had been intended to be: A showcase for amateur athletics, something people did in addition to doing something else. Athletes trained at night, after they had worked all day.

"Running was something I had done. Period," says Quinn. "I didn't dwell on it."

"Did people know that you had won a gold medal?"

"I didn't tell them," he says. "Sometimes I think I was embarrassed about it. I really don't like to be prominent. It's my nature to stay in the background. The last thing I wanted to be was some old guy talking about how he used to be a great runner."

Said his wife: "I was married to him for 20 years before I knew he had a gold medal."

For years, Quinn didn't even know where the gold medal was. He'd figured he'd lost it until finding it one day in a closet. Even now, there are few mementos of his career. Just a few old clippings and a lamp that was made out of a silver cup he got from the New

York Athletic Club when he broke the world record in the 60-yard dash.

Which is why he looks at the recent attention he's been receiving with a certain bemusement. He knows it's because of his longevity, the fact he's become the oldest American to have won a gold medal, beating out a teammate from that '28 Olympic team by eight months. After all, he's lived years and years in obscurity, not even his neighbors knowing that the quiet, unassuming man down the street once won one of the biggest sports awards of all, a gold medal at the Olympics.

"But it's nice to be recognized before they plant me down," Quinn says with a laugh.

Now he watches the Olympics on television, even though he knows they are so different from back in Amsterdam in 1928. He says he doesn't regret the fact that if he'd born in a different era his life might have been different more money, more fame.

"I don't regret that," says Jim Quinn. "I had my time."

Yes, he did.

His gold medal tells us that.

ED DUCKWORTH

2001

"What can I say? We were maroons."

—Ed Duckworth

PROVIDENCE — I have an enduring image of Ed Duckworth, who just retired after 38 years at the Providence Journal.

He is sitting in the sports department and his feet are up on the desk. He is, of course, puffing on a cigar. He is talking about how the Red Sox stink, the Pats stink, all of the local teams stink. Everything stinks.

It's the early '80s, he is the assistant sports editor, and if you were looking to film a remake of The Front Page, Duckworth would have been sent over from Central Casting.

Rest assured, Damon Runyon couldn't have made him up.

Or who buys the left-behind clothes of people who recently died, then comes into the office to show off the great deal he'd gotten?

Then there was the time he was at a Bruins game and called the office.

"Where are your pre-game notes?" the night editor asked.

"When the guy from Hartford comes up and gives his to me, then you'll get them," Duckworth said. "Some might call it plagiarism. I tend to look at it more as research."

Welcome to Sports Writing 101, the kind they don't teach in the journalism schools.

But don't be fooled by the act. In his own idiosyncratic way, Duckworth was the consummate pro. He could cover anything, he could flat out write and he could always make deadline. If the world was going to end and you needed someone to cover it, you'd send Duckworth. Because he'd get it right.

Sports writing is a different business now. Everyone has a laptop. No one comes into the office. Even when they do, it's a very different place. The sports department no longer is a glorified locker room the way it used to be when Duckworth sat with his feet up on the desk, puffing on his cigar.

But Duckworth never changed. In a sense he was the last remnant from a gone-forever time. A time when Brown football led the sports page every autumn Sunday, and every Sunday night the Reds played in the auditorium on North Main Street, the old barn where guys took book in the lobby, and the cigar smoke seemed to hang over the ice like coastal fog.

This was Duckworth's world, a place where big fights were still king, and horse racing was still all over the sports page. A world of small-time hustlers and wise guys who always gave you tips that ran out of the money. Back before gender equity and political correctness. Back before money corrupted sports and a lot of fun went out of the sports writing business.

He had grown up in Providence, went to Hope High School, then Boston University. He arrived here in the sports department in the early '60s. Suffice to say he's seen the comet of change that's the newspaper business.

"Name me one thing that's better today than it was 30 years ago," he challenged me one day. "Name one. Music's worse. Movies are worse. Cars are worse. Sports are worse. Everything's worse."

But if there was a lament for the ways things used to be, Duckworth always could laugh at himself, too.

Like the time he was covering the second Vinny Pazienza-Greg Haugen fight in Atlantic City, a fight Haugen won. Seems Duckworth had predicted Paz would win, a story Haugen had obviously read. So when Haugen and his entourage came into the casino later that night there was Duckworth standing right in front of him.

"Hey Duckworth!" Haugen yelled. Then he made an obscene gesture.

No one laughed harder than Duckworth.

Or the story he told about himself and actress Faye Dunaway. Seems they had gone to BU together, had been part of the same card group, Dunaway being the only woman. But she had been a little heavier then, not the glamorous woman who only a few years later would explode across the screen in Bonnie and Clyde. So no one ever asked her out. No one ever paid her any real attention. To Duckworth and his card buddies, she was just one of the guys.

"What can I say?" he said. "We were maroons," a word he'd concocted from "moron," and "buffoon."

In the end, in Duckworth's view, we were all "maroons." Him, me, all of us who still do this for a living. As if we all had stayed too long at the dance, and now the music was over, all the good people had gone home, and all that was left were the memories.

He had grown up with hockey, but his real love was horse racing. To see him at the race track was like seeing Sinatra with a microphone in his hand. The bets. The one-liners. The cigar. It was all timeless, Oscar Madison right here in the Journal sports department.

"They're off, you lose," he always used to say, mimicking a racetrack announcer. "They're off, you lose again."

A horse player's credo.

"How's the new computer?" I asked one day, seeing him with one of those state-of-the-art machines that almost seem able to talk.

"Too much horse," he said.

On his last day of work we were at Foxboro Stadium together. It was a Monday, and we were in the Patriots locker room. He was saying how he and his wife were moving to Florida, to a beach town near a racetrack, and I was thinking of how different it will be around here when he's gone, about how much I will miss him. About how sports departments go on, but eras end.

A few of the Patriots sat in front of their lockers.

"Hey, Margie," Duckworth called over to another reporter in the room . . . "I'll give you 20 bucks if you get me three quotes."

Like I said, they don't teach that at journalism school.

TWO BROTHERS, ONE SECOND CHANCE

2002

"I will do anything not to mess this up."

—Deon Anderson

STORRS, Conn. — His world was a simpler place the first time I met Deon Anderson.

It was in the fall of 1998 at Portsmouth Abbey, the prestigious prep school that speaks of money and success, its sloping green lawns so often an escalator to golden futures. Deon Anderson was the kid from South Providence whose football talent was one day going to take him to big stadiums and Saturday afternoon cheers.

"He is the kind of athlete we don't get here," said Peter Mack, then the school's athletic director. "We could go 20 years and never have another Deon Anderson."

Anderson had grown up off Broad Street in South Providence, and the first time he saw Portsmouth Abbey, with its trees and green grass and campus that looks out over the ocean, it was as though he had been dropped on some other planet. He was 14 years old, and the first thing he did was go to his dorm room and cry.

On the surface, he was an inner-city stereotype, one of three kids essentially raised by his grandmother in the kind of neighborhood where too many futures shrink before their time. But he had been fortunate, too. His family had stressed education. He had gone to elementary school at San Miguel in Providence, a small private school that had prepared him academically for Portsmouth Abbey.

And it wasn't long before he realized the opportunity that lay in front of him. He saw too many of the kids back in the old neighborhood getting in trouble, too many kids who had either already quit school, or were thinking of it. Too many kids whose worlds were shrinking.

The night I met him, Anderson couldn't have been happier, complete with a smile that lit up the room. Everything seemed to fit. He knew how fortunate he was to be where he was. Football was only a part of it, even if it did promise to one day take him far from the prep school fields he played on. But two years later, he was sent back home to Providence, the result of a campus incident, the details of which remain sketchy.

"All I did was cry," Anderson said. "I would sit in my room and not come out. I stayed in my room for three weeks. I was devastated. I had loved Portsmouth Abbey."

Eventually, he went to Hope High School. He always had prided himself on his will and determination. He would make a comeback. He did well in school. He played basketball. He ran track. He tried to fit in, to get along with people, as he always had.

But all around him he saw the fights and the constant chaos at Hope. He knew that if you were from the south side of the city you weren't supposed to go in certain parts of the building, the unofficial street code of the school, as if the school was made up of small duchies, each one fearful of the others. He saw the kids who didn't do any homework, the ones who didn't care. He had been to one of the most prestigious prep schools in the country and the more time he spent at Hope the more he knew what he'd left behind.

"I knew I had had the opportunity of a lifetime at Portsmouth Abbey and had thrown it all away," he said.

The second body blow came in June of 2000, the night he heard that his older brother Raymond had been arrested.

"I thought it was for something silly," he said. "Like breaking a window, or smoking some weed."

It was not. It was for the car-jack murders of two college students, a horrific crime that shocked the state. Raymond Anderson, who had dropped out of school in the 10th grade, was one of five young men charged with the crime. Last January, he admitted his guilt in federal court, a plea agreement that could reduce his federal sentencing. Afterward, his attorney said Raymond Anderson was "extremely remorseful" about his part in the murders.

By then, though, Deon Anderson was worlds away.

He had been given another chance. It was at Avon Old Farms, a Connecticut prep school where he went in the fall of 2000 to try and rebuild both his life and his football career. Once again, he ran through opponents the way he once had at Portsmouth Abbey, as if running for his future. Once again, he quickly demonstrated he was a definite college prospect, eventually recruited by numerous universities. He was at Avon for two years.

Anderson chose the University of Connecticut, the old Yankee Conference school that now plays Division 1-A football, the only New England school besides Boston College that does so. He also became one of the few Rhode Islanders in recent years to be given a Division I-A scholarship, fulfilling the promise he had shown back at Portsmouth Abbey, back when his coach said that one day Anderson would be a big-time college football player.

So there he was the other afternoon, sitting outside the UConn locker room, almost four years from that first time I'd met him. Still stocky, with 217 pounds on a 6-foot frame. Still looking like he could drag a linebacker into the end zone. Still with a big smile.

And smile he should.

He is the starting fullback, even though he's only a freshman. In his first game, he scored a touchdown against Boston College. He is a good young player on an up-and-coming team, one that's scheduled to play next year in a new 40,000-seat stadium in Hartford, a good young player at a school that now has big-time football aspirations.

"I love it here," he said. "I felt comfortable from the first time I visited."

He said he almost went to an Ivy League school, but UConn just felt like a better fit. He said he wants to be an architect, either that or work on Wall Street. He said he takes school seriously, not just football.

I asked him if he had learned anything from what happened to his brother.

"I made a mistake at Portsmouth Abbey," he said quietly, "but my brother made a big mistake. He showed me that one mistake can ruin your life."

He hesitated a beat, stared off into space.

"I would have bet my life that my brother wouldn't have been involved in anything like that," he said. "He's not like that. But he made an awful decision, then things got out of control . . . "

His voice trailed off.

He said how he writes his brother almost every day, visits him in jail when he can.

"He's become my motivation," Anderson said, as if he now lives for both of them.

He looks at his teammates as they come out of the locker room on a glorious September afternoon, at the UConn campus that bustles with life and energy, at the opportunity that now lies in front of him like a promise.

"I will not mess this up," says Deon Anderson. "Never, never. Never that. I will do anything not to mess this up."

Courtesy of Brown University

MARVELOUS MEMORIES

2002

"How could you guys win? You're awful."

PROVIDENCE — One of the equipment men actually lived there for a couple years, bunking in the basement behind a meshed screen with his girlfriend and a dog named Marvel.

One of the trainers once became irate after Brown upset URI because he had bet on the Rams, berating us with, "How could you guys win? You're awful."

When we practiced, the freshman team was on a court on one side, intramurals were on another, the track team was running overhead, and invariably some guy was kicking a soccer ball in the corner. Every time we played Providence College in the '60s, the gym would be jam-packed with people, so loud you could almost hear the old walls shake, an unbelievable atmosphere. The only problem was the overwhelming majority of people were rooting for the Friars.

Ah, Marvel Gym.

I was thinking of all that the other day while riding by what used to be Marvel, thinking of how I saw my first college basketball game there in the '50s when I was 10 years old, thinking how many years of my life I had spent there. Thinking of how important it was to me, my own little field of dreams. Thinking of how few things make you feel the passage of time like seeing one of the citadels of your past crumbling in front of you.

For Marvel is being demolished now, the insides all but gutted, just the husk remaining.

And the memories.

Like the night in March of '67 when Jimmy Walker walked in just five minutes before the game, then led PC to victory. Or the night in 1970 when a group of black students walked on the court in the middle of a game to protest some campus issue. Or in the early '70s when the black students would sit on one side of the court and the whites on the other, all you had to know about race in America at the time.

Or in 1978, when the Penn team was brought in by National Guard trucks in the aftermath of the famous blizzard, and people walked through the snow-clogged streets of the East Side to go to the game. Or like the times trainer Eddie Jamiel played the national anthem on his trumpet.

Marvel.

Where anything could happen.

And usually did.

It opened in December of 1927, hailed as "one of the most complete indoor facilities in the country." It was four stories, red brick, a showplace. It was called the Brown Gymnasium then, and it was part of a complex that had the football stadium across Elmgrove Avenue and numerous playing fields next to it. It became Marvel a decade later, named after a longtime athletic director. And Marvel it remained, an East Side institution.

During World War II, areas around Marvel were made available to Brown employees for victory gardens. After the war, a housing complex for veterans was built on land where the Jewish Community Center now stands. For five years, several barracks from Newport were brought in and 100 families lived there. It was called "Brown Town."

But of course I knew none of that as a Brown basketball player in the '60s. All I knew was that by then Marvel spoke more about college basketball's past than it did of its future, already a monument to another era. It had hissing pipes, rafters in the ceiling, a skylight, and a catwalk that went all the way to the top of the building. It had a running track that circled overhead, complete with people hanging over the railing.

And I also knew I loved playing there. It was small, it was dark, the people were right on top of you. It was always a gym, never an arena. A place where you could almost smell the tradition, right there with the popcorn being sold by the court. A place where you could almost reach out and touch the soul of college basketball, before it became glitzy.

Marvel.

You couldn't make it up.

When Brown opened its new Pizzitola Center in 1989, there was talk that Marvel would become condos. Then it was going to be used for storage. Eventually, it just sat there, the windows broken, the years going by. The statue of the brown bear that used to stand in front, under which generations of Brown football captains were photographed, was moved to the campus. But Marvel continued to sit there in the darkness on Elmgrove Avenue, more and more about the past, just another piece of old Rhode Island drifting away.

To me, though, it still was there. I drove by it. I saw it across the street at Brown football games. I could close my eyes and still see Marvel the way it used to be, back when so much of my life seemed to revolve around it. From a distance, it still looked like it always did, and that was somehow comforting.

Now it's being razed, the land to be used for intramural playing fields. Soon, it will exist only in memory, another reminder that nothing lasts forever, not even the echoes of old cheers. They say there's going to be a plaque where the statue of the bear used to be, right in front of where Marvel was, telling people what used to be there.

It's going to take a big plaque.

FOOT SOLDIER FOR PEACE— CEDRIC HUNTLEY

2003

"If we don't help these kids, who is going to?"

—Cedric Huntley

PROVIDENCE — Maybe it's because he's been to too many funerals.

Or maybe it was the realization that too many kids are getting shot here, too many are dying. Maybe it was the simple realization that if this was happening in Cranston or Warwick, neighborhoods where white kids live, there would be a public outcry. Or maybe it was the simple fact that too many of the kids reminded him of himself 25 years ago.

But somewhere along the way Cedric Huntley decided to try to do something about it.

"This has become my life," he said. "This is what I do."

Once he was a high school basketball star. The time was the late 1970s. The place was La Salle Academy. Back then, he and his older brother Chris were two of the first African-American basketball stars at La Salle. He had come out of the Roger Williams housing project on Public Street in South Providence, had grown up in an era of racial turmoil, had grown up "with the violence, the riots, the whole nine yards."

Basketball had done a lot to keep him away from much of the trouble. The game was his escape, his sanctuary. It indirectly got him to La Salle, which opened up the world for him, gave him opportunities and possibilities that didn't exist in the housing project. It helped him get to CCRI, after his dream of playing big-time college basketball had ended. For Huntley was like a lot of inner-city kids then. He thought he was one day going to play in the NBA, thought basketball always was going to be some passport to fame and fortune, the ghetto fairy tale.

But this is not some lament about a dream that died, not about someone who couldn't find a second act once the ball stopped bouncing. It's just the opposite. This is about someone who has come back to the neighborhood that spawned him, come back to this place where the so-called Providence Renaissance seems very far away, come back to be a foot soldier in what's become an ongoing war.

"This is where my roots are," he said. "My passion is here."

Friday morning he was in the gym at the Met, a charter school on Public Street that sits like a jewel in a neighborhood where the seeds of too many dreams never get to flourish. Huntley is the athletic director here, but that's only part of what he does. He is also the director at the South Providence Recreation Center. And he is one of three voluntary coordinators of a program that sends eight street workers into the city's most troubled neighborhoods in an attempt to diffuse tensions and try to keep things from spilling over to the kind of violence that leads to too many funerals.

"It's all connected," he said. "So many of the kids I deal with in school are the same kids I deal with at night."

He has just come out of a meeting with a kid who feels pressure to join a gang. He talks about another kid who is in a crisis situation. These are all scenes from the larger story of neighborhood feuds and escalating violence, the ongoing battle to try to save a generation.

This is the Providence that's not part of Water Fire and gondola rides and the fancy restaurants that live off people from the suburbs. The Providence that has nothing to do with moving rivers and building new hotels in search of the tourist buck. This is the Providence of sirens and the sound of gunshots in the night, of kids who live in fear, of gritty streets where there are too many drugs, too many gangs, too many guns, and too little hope that it's ever going to change. The Providence that got left behind.

Thursday night had been another reminder. Another night of someone getting shot in the neighborhood. Another night of someone else getting stabbed. Another night in the mosaic of violence and broken dreams that have become life here in the inner-city. Another night in Huntley's life.

"When things are really poppin', we're out every night," he said.

This is said with no bravado, simply as a statement of fact. Huntley is low key, goes out of his way to say he's not the only one doing this, simply part of a group that's trying to stem what he sees as an epidemic of violence. He specifically mentions Teny Gross, the director of the Institute for the Study and Practice of Non-violence in South Providence, who helped start the street-workers program in early August, and George Lindsay, another co-coordinator.

"I wouldn't want to be a young person living in this city now," Huntley said. "It's so much worse than when I was a kid, and it wasn't good then."

So where does a social conscience come from?

It could have been when he was 14 or so and spent a summer working at a camp for kids with special needs. Or growing up and hearing the older folks talk about Martin Luther King. Or when he realized that he got the opportunity to go to La Salle because a priest he didn't even know paid his way, or the belief that everyone needs some help along the way. Maybe it was the realization when he was about 20 that he didn't want to be defined by just being a basketball player, that there were more important arenas to play in.

But somewhere Huntley realized he had something he wanted to do to help these kids, the kids who remind him of who he used to be.

"All it's about for these young people is someone to stop and listen to them," he said. "And to be there."

That's the goal of the street-workers program. Be a presence.

Do interventions. Do all the behind-the-scenes work that doesn't get headlines, but just might prevent them.

And Huntley knows sports can have a role in this, too. Certainly it did in his own life. Sports have the power to cross boundaries, to serve as common ground, and it's in this role as peacemaker that there's going to be a one-day basketball tournament at the Dunkin' Donuts Center on Oct. 19. It's being called the first annual "P-Town Basketball Classic For Peace" and it's going to bring kids from the different neighborhoods together.

It's a step.

And, as Huntley believes, it's all interrelated: The more kids who realize that there are people who know them, care about them, are there for them, the fewer funerals there are going to be. For he's come to believe that the solutions to the city's problems lie in the community itself. With people who live and work here. With people who know the families, the histories. With people who are here day after day, the thread that helps makes up the community's fabric.

He knows how fragile it all is, how kids' lives can change in an instant. Joining a gang. Selling some drugs because everyone else is doing it. Or else some foolish retribution for some perceived slight, the sense that if you don't retaliate then you're only getting "dissed" and there's nothing worse than that, right? Lives that can hinge on one bad decision. All played out against a backdrop of poverty and too many broken families. The daily minefield so many of these kids walk through.

"If we don't help these kids, who is going to?" he asked. "This is our responsibility."

He paused a second. And when he spoke again his voice seemed to come up through layers of resolve.

"When I was coming along there were a lot of people along the way that pointed me in the right direction," said Cedric Huntley. "Now it's my turn to try to do some of the pointing."

FOR 30 YEARS, PARRILLO LED THE FIELD

2003

PROVIDENCE — I have an enduring image of Bill Parrillo, who died late Friday night.

It is right here in the sports department of the Providence Journal newsroom, deadline quickly approaching. Parrillo is at a desk that's covered with notes, personal hieroglyphics that look impossible to decipher. He is wearing some horrible golf sweater that he got from some pro-am tournament somewhere. He's working on a column, and it's obvious he's in trouble, in some personal maze he's unable to extricate himself from.

As usual, he is behind schedule. As usual, editors on the desk are screaming for the column. As usual, he is ignoring them. And I think he's not going to be able to finish this one, that there's no way he's going to make deadline and be in tomorrow's newspaper. I watch him struggle and I think, this is finally the time he's got himself into a hole even he can't get out of.

Once again, I am wrong.

Bill Parrillo was always in tomorrow's newspaper.

Always.

He worked here for 40 years, wrote a column for nearly 30 of those years. Day after day. Week after week. Year after year. As presidents changed, music changed, sports changed, everything changed. Somehow Parrillo never did. The consummate pro, in his own idiosyncratic way. He covered the Olympics. He covered the World Series. He covered Super Bowls. He covered the Pats and the Red Sox and just about everything else for that matter. He did columns on big people, little people, all kinds of people.

He wrote and filed a column in darkness after an earthquake hit San Francisco moments before a World Series game. He also did a column about the doctors and nurses who brought him back to health after he had internal bleeding in 1994. In short, he could write about anything.

A pro.

He was also a giant here at the Providence Journal, a sports columnist at a time when there was only one. He took over that role from John Hanlon in 1974, when the sports world was a different place. No talk radio. Few opinion pieces on the sports page. No Internet, with its chat rooms full of self-proclaimed experts. In a sense, the columnist was the only voice back then, and for a generation of Rhode Islanders who followed sports, Parrillo was that voice.

Always measured. Never confrontational. The voice of someone who had grown up in Johnston, played football at Mount Pleasant High School, graduated URI, knew sports around here as well as anyone ever has. The voice of someone over the backyard fence who had access to things you didn't. That was Parrillo's style. He took you into the post-game locker room. He got you closer to things. He set the scene, and put the reader in it. Most of all, he put things in perspective. Both about sports, and the people who play them.

"When I came home from school, he was the guy I read," says colleague Kevin McNamara, who grew up in Coventry in the '70s.

But it was never easy. Seeing Parrillo work told you that. He labored over columns, changing this, adding that, always looking for another word, another phrase, something to make them better. Back when he wrote for the old Evening Bulletin, an afternoon paper, he would sometimes take all night to finish his column, ending up in the sports department by himself in the wee hours of the morning, sitting there in his stockinged feet and ugly golf sweater as dawn crept through the windows.

And in a business that's more and more about attitude, more and more about self-promotion, more and more about style over substance, Parrillo was a throwback in the very best sense of the word. He didn't want to be on TV. He didn't want to do radio. He wanted to write his column. And that's what he did. Day after day. Week after week. Year after year.

The amazing thing was he never lost his passion for it. In retrospect, that was his great gift to all of us. The years would change, we'd all get older, more jaded, yet Parrillo's enthusiasm for the job never wavered. Even in the past few years, when he had both a liver transplant and a kidney transplant, had seen his own mortality, he kept working. Not because he had to. Because he wanted to. Until November 2001, when he covered the Pats and Rams at Foxboro Stadium, the last column he ever did.

Parrillo was a private man in a public job, so maybe it's not surprising that he spoke little about his health problems. He said he didn't want people to feel sorry for him, worry about him. Until recently, he was still hoping to come back to work, for he didn't like the way his career had ended, no goodbye, no farewell, just over, like a game that ran out of time. His wife, Mary, said the other night that even in the past year, between treatments and fighting his illness, he would look at the sports section every morning and say what he would have written. As if 40 years, and all those words, hadn't been enough.

Vintage Bill Parrillo.

The only things missing were the notes on the desk and the deadlines.

BRITTO'S IMMORTALITY IS FIRMLY ROOTED IN FOX POINT

2003

"I've got no regrets. That was my time."

—John Britto

PROVIDENCE — I am here in search of a little Rhode Island sports history.

The place is the Fox Point Boys and Girls Club. The guy I'm here to see is John Britto. Who is John Britto? He might just be one of this state's great sports secrets.

Or how many other Rhode Islanders once played for the Harlem Globetrotters?

"Johnny Britto was a great player," says Vin Cullen, the longtime coach at CCRI who played against Britto in local leagues. "He was a magician with the ball."

The only problem was not many people knew that back in the mid-1950s. Back then, there were only a handful of blacks in the NBA, never mind college basketball. In most ways, basketball was a white game then, opportunities for black players as rare as sneaker contracts. And they certainly didn't exist for Britto, whose parents had arrived here by ship from the Cape Verde Islands, settling in Fox Point because there already was a Cape Verdean population there.

Britto was the fifth of nine children, and if there was never enough money, that really wasn't the end of the world then because no one he saw around him had any money, either. Cape Verdeans.

Portuguese. Irish. Lebanese. They all were in Fox Point then, one big ethnic stew. And to Britto, everyone always got along.

"They used to say at Hope High School that there were three groups," he says. "Black. White. And Fox Point. I always liked that, because that's the way it was."

Britto was just a kid when his father died, and much of his youth was spent in the old Boys Club on the corner of South Main and Power streets. He lived across the street, in a cold-water flat that was always too hot in the summer and too cold in the winter, and his mother was forever sending him to the Boys Club, into a world where sports was king.

It was an era when everyone seemed to know everyone, one in which the last thing in the world you wanted to do was bring shame on your family. An era when the neighborhood ruled. Few people ever loved Fox Point any more than Britto did. So when he came back from Korea and got a chance to join a basketball team from the neighborhood, that's what he did.

It was called the AGMACs, and it was named in honor of Antonio Gomes, a neighborhood kid who had died in Korea: The Antonio Gomes Memorial Athletic Club. The AGMACs played in all the local leagues back then, and on weekends they would pile into somebody's old car and barnstorm around New England. Sometimes they would even go to New York and New Jersey, and sometimes they would even make a few bucks. They were virtually an all-black team then, but not always.

And they would play against anybody.

"We were the biggest name in basketball at the time," Britto says. "And just the name alone made it an honor to play for the AGMACs."

"The Rhode Island League then was full of very good players," Cullen says. "Jimmy Adams. Slick Pina. Leon Harris. Vinnie Britto. Phil Jones, who played for the Westerly team and was the captain at UConn. But I always thought Johnny Britto was the best. He was about 6-foot-3, which was big back then, and he could really handle the ball. Just a super, super player."

By the mid-'50s, the word was out on Britto, to the point that a scout for the Harlem Globetrotters came to see him play. The Globetrotters were the most popular basketball team in the world at the time, were less than a decade removed from beating George Mikan and the Minneapolis Lakers for the unofficial world title, and in an NBA that offered very few opportunities for black players, the Globetrotters were the pinnacle.

Britto played with the Globetrotters for a year. Although they were called the Harlem Globetrotters, their home base was Chicago, and the reality was that every night there was another game in a different place. The star was Meadowlark Lemon, called the clown prince of basketball, and Britto was one of the extras. He loved the life, and for a Cape Verdean kid from Fox Point, he knew he was never going to go any higher in sports than this. But he was newly married and knew his real life was back in Rhode Island, not doing tricks with the Globetrotters, even if he was a magician with the ball. So he came home.

Back to Fox Point.

He continued to play for the AGMACs through the '50s, eventually playing against all the local college players. He was the first black to play for Local 57, then the state's fast-pitch softball team. He played in the Amateur League in baseball until he was 39.

"I came in on a ball one day, the ball went over my head, and I just kept on running to the bench," he says. "I knew I was done."

He is 70 now, but you still can't keep Britto out of the Fox Point Boys and Girls Club. His title is physical education director, but titles don't tell any of it. He really is the club's soul, always here, day after day, year after year, as the little kids grow up and then come back with their own little kids. He's been here for almost 30 years now, the one who always seems to have a conga line of kids trailing after him, calling him Johnny, just as their parents did before them.

But even that doesn't tell the entire story. It doesn't tell about all the times he's given kids rides home, or all the youth teams he's coached for no money, the endless hours he still puts in. Or that, to many, he's long been "Mr. Fox Point." Nor does it tell the story of his basketball career, and a lost era that now only exists in the memories of old men.

"I hear you were good," I say to Britto.

He looks at me, then looks away.

"I was all right," he says dismissively. "A lot of guys were just as good."

Not really.

But Britto's not going to say that. He will tell you, though, about how much he loved the AGMACs, how sweetly he remembers the time. And if he knows that it all might have been different if he had come along later, that his basketball talent might have taken him places he couldn't have imagined back then, it's not something he dwells on. In fact, it's just the opposite. For he feels he came of age in what was, in many ways, a better time. One of family and respect and a nurturing neighborhood. A neighborhood where everyone got along. A way of life that has all but disappeared.

"I've got no regrets," he says. "That was my time."

One that received a certain immortality Friday night when John Britto was inducted into the New England Basketball Hall of Fame.

NICK'S: A REFUGE THROUGH WAR AND PEACE

2003

"It was like stepping into a time capsule..."

—Bill Reynolds

BARRINGTON — The walls already are bare.

The memorabilia has been packed away, 38 years put in boxes. The only thing left is the full-length picture of Kevin McHale in his uniform in the Celtics' glory days. That, and a photocopy from a 1918 Boston Globe story saying the Red Sox had won the championship. And tomorrow Nick Conti is going to close the door for the last time in the barbershop he and his brother Lou have run since Lyndon Johnson was in the White House.

He's also going to close the door on a slice of my past.

Once upon a time, back in the 1960s, the shop was my sanctuary. It was like stepping into a time capsule, a place far removed from burning cities and Sgt. Pepper and an America that seemed to be coming apart. A place where the biggest issue of the day was the pennant race, not the human race. A place where you could listen to arguments about who had been the best athletes in Bristol County, circa 1952.

It was a slice of small-town life, one of those places where people knew your name. No small thing in Barrington then, a town that seemed to be changing as quickly as the country.

Its official name was the County Road Barbershop, but no one ever called it that. It was just the barbershop. Or Nick's. And the great thing about it was it was always there. Day after day. Month after month. Year after year. The world kept spinning, everything kept changing, but inside the shop it was timeless. Or so it seemed to me.

In a way it was out of place in Barrington. Nick's was one of those places that could have been in some Pennsylvania steel town that genuflected to high-school football. Either that, or some blue-collar New England mill town where sports were the lifeblood. On the surface, it was an incongruity in a suburban town, especially one that often seemed to be so consumed with appearances. For it was never a salon. It was a barbershop, complete with hair on the floor and sports pictures on the walls. There was one of Tony Conigliaro. There was one of Mickey Mantle. There was the baseball encyclopedia, the official arbiter of all baseball trivia arguments.

The Conti brothers were from Bristol. Nick was the industrious one, the one who worried about how many customers were walking through the door. Lou was the one who put the magazine over his face, pretending he didn't see the customer coming into the store, making Nick cut another head.

And then there was Jack.

He was about 30 then, sat in the barbershop every day. He originally was from Cleveland and the Indians were his obsession. One day, several years before, he'd been on his way to Boston to finish a college career that had been interrupted by a four-year hitch in the Air Force. He stopped for a haircut, got into an argument about the Indians, and never left.

Every morning around 10 he would arrive in his red and white Corvette, walk in with his blue blazer as if he were on the way to some cushy job in Providence, hang up the blazer, and hold court for the next five hours. He argued sports with Nick and Lou. He kibbitzed with the customers. He became the sideshow. Then at 3 o'clock he went home to watch Leave it to Beaver reruns and have afternoon cocktails. Every day. Year after year.

Jack's long gone now, but there still was an Indians hat over the chair where he always sat. Through the years others have come and gone, guys for whom the barbershop became their hangout, before time and circumstance took them away. Like the guy who couldn't speak who used to wash the windows in exchange for haircuts. Like Louie "Coke," so named because he once worked for Coca Cola. Like the others who have been coming here for years, tradition in a town that's become transient.

Nick is 64 now, his brother a year older, and he says it's time. He's also been cutting hair at the veterans' home in Bristol in the mornings for a while now, and no longer wants to do two jobs.

"I don't want to be standing next to this chair when I'm 80," he said the other morning. "I don't want any longevity records."

Take away the bare walls and the boxes on the floor, and it could have been any year. The radio was tuned to 790 The Score. There were a handful of guys waiting for haircuts, A hand-written sign said haircuts were six bucks. Outside the window, on County Road, it was 2003. But inside? Timeless.

The other day a reporter from a local paper came in to do a story.

"I've been here 38 years," Nick said, "and now I won't be anymore. What more do you want to know?"

Ah, but there's so much more to know.

Like how Nick once played on a state championship Little League team from Bristol in 1952, how he learned firsthand that sometimes sports never get any better than they are when you're 12 years old. How he used to idolize Johnny Egan, back when it was all beginning for Providence College basketball. How he used to count Mickey Mantle's home runs. How he's been here in this place cutting hair and talking sports for 38 years now, one of the few constants in a world that rushes by outside the window.

"What's it going to be like the last time you walk out of here?" I asked.

He paused a beat, as if running all the years quickly through his head, all the memories, all the laughs, all the people, a time gone by.

"Sure, I'm going to miss it," he said.

Me too, Nick. Me too.

JIMMY BURCHFIELD'S GOOD FIGHT

2004

"Anything I do, I try to be the best at."
—Jimmy Burchfield

NORTH PROVIDENCE — He's been around for a while now, as Rhode Island as frozen lemonade and day trips to the beach. Our own version of Damon Runyon, a throwback to some lost time of ring girls and fight nights where the smoke hung over the ring like gauze and wise-guys in shiny suits sat in the front row with dames on their arms.

Boxing as romance.

Jimmy Burchfield presents . . . Jimmy Burchfield's Classic Restaurant . . . Jimmy Burchfield in a black tuxedo, standing in the ring at Foxwoods and kissing Vinny Paz a few weeks after Paz's last fight . . . A Jimmy Burchfield production.

But who is Jimmy Burchfield? And how did he get from nowhere to somewhere? How did he become the local fight promoter, the man who kept the sport alive around here in the waning years of Paz's career, the man who has turned local boxing into a sort of cottage industry? The man who will promote a night of boxing next Friday at the Convention Center, one that will be televised on ESPN? This man who says his Classic Entertainment Sports has become a franchise around here, "like the Pawtucket Red Sox and the Providence Bruins."

Who is he?

The pictures are your first clue. They are all over the walls of this small office on Charles Street, a mini-Hall of Fame. Pictures of Vinny Paz and Sugar Ray Leonard. Pictures of Rocky Marciano and Muhammad Ali. Pictures of Joe Frazier. Pictures of Tommy Lasorda and Dan Marino. Pictures of innumerable boxers staring down from the walls. Pictures of fighters who have come and gone. Pictures. The snapshots of Jimmy Burchfield's life. In the neighborhood that both defined him and nurtured him.

For that's all a part of this. It might even be the most important part. The neighborhood. Charles Street in Providence in the '50s, blue collar, Italian, working class. The kind of neighborhood where you used to hang on the corner of Charles Street and Mineral Spring Avenue until the cops came and chased everyone away.

"You had to fight to survive," Jimmy Burchfield says. "And in that neighborhood, you either went south or north."

He went north. Away from the trouble and the guys who flirted with the law. Away from the guys who hung on the corner like kindling just waiting for a match. Maybe that was because he always was a little different, the Italian kid with the English last name, courtesy of his stepfather, the man Burchfield was raised by, the one he calls father. Maybe it was because his grandparents had a welding company he used to work at, and he grew up hearing his grandfather's voice in his head, words that said "Work hard . . . Do what you say you're going to do . . . Stand with your head up straight."

"I saw a lot of guys I grew up with get in trouble, a lot of guys overdose," Burchfield says.

He went to North Providence High School, played football and baseball. Afterwards, he played softball in local leagues. He went to work in a lumber yard in West Warwick, owned by a man named Clarence Couto, who became his mentor. Burchfield eventually ending up running the lumber yard because, to him, "Anything I do, I try to be the best at it."

It was the same attitude he brought to a small bar he bought on Charles Street. It was just a neighborhood place then, but from the beginning Burchfield brought the same work ethic he later would bring to Classic Entertainment Sports. He cooked. He bartended. He cleaned tables. Some nights, in the beginning, he did all those things and at the end of the night he had something like five dollars in his pocket. It took three years to make it work. He eventually turned a small mom-and-pop restaurant into a Vegas-style supper club, doing the transformation in four and a half days.

Those were the days. Jimmy Burchfield's Classic Restaurant. One night Dan Marino stopped in. Another, in came Sugar Ray Leonard. Ali himself came in, ended up bartending, a woman fainting when she asked for a drink and realized who was serving it to her. It also was where Burchfield first met Vinny Paz.

It was the '80s, the young fighter from Cranston beginning to make a name for himself, all but becoming boxing, itself, in a state where the sport virtually had ceased to exist. So one night Burchfield wrote him a letter, invited him to the Classic. That was the beginning of both his relationship with Paz and his career as a promoter. Burchfield had been both a boxing referee and a judge. Eventually, he became an international judge, working fights around the world. Now, with his friendship with Paz, he became a promoter too. His first show was at Rocky Point in the '80s.

"It was a complete flop," Burchfield says.

Now he's done close to 150 events, and he's no longer in the restaurant business. He's done them here and he's done them there. At Foxwoods. Around the country. He even did one once at the Melody Tent on the Cape, where a skunk was trapped underneath the makeshift ring for the entire night. He now has 33 fighters, 18 of them local. Seven will fight Friday night at the Convention Center, a card called "Young Guns," featuring Peter Manfredo Jr. of Providence.

"We are a player," Burchfield says, "and we're not going away. How many other events in Rhode Island are on ESPN?"

But it's not always easy. The fight business can be as byzantine as a medieval duchy, a world where many of the inhabitants seem to have more teeth than a hungry shark. It's also not always easy promoting fights in Rhode Island, where he sometimes feels like he's rowing a boat against the current. There's little margin of error; you're only as good as your last promotion.

"It's easier to go to the casinos," he says. "But this is my state. This is my hometown. This is where I live. And if Rhode Island wants big-time boxing, I can supply it. We'll see if it wants it. But we've got real fighters. We play real games. And we've got the talent to go to the major leagues."

That remains to be seen.

But he's 62 now, and there's no question he's come so very far from the Charles Street of his youth, and has had the kind of success he never could have imagined back there in the '50s, back when opportunities could seem so limited. He has become a player on the local sports scene, and he has done it his way, one promotion after another, year after year, until he's become one of those names everyone knows, even if they don't always know the particulars.

And that corner where he used to be run off, the one where Mineral Spring Avenue cuts across Charles Street?

He owns it.

"Only in America," he says with a smile.

Damon Runyon lives.

Either that, or he's become just another Jimmy Burchfield production.

EMIL JOHN

1990

"I see love in them and it arouses love in me. That is the reward."

—EMIL JOHN

PROVIDENCE — He has worked here in the sports department at the Providence Journal for more than 30 years, but that's never really been Emil John's work.

The real work has been at Trinity United Methodist Church on Broad Street in Providence, right in the middle of the inner city, a place that's become a euphemism for too many crushed hopes and broken dreams. He has been the church's minister. He's been the assistant minister. He's typed the church's newsletters, and worked the soup kitchens and served on this committee and that committee. For more than 20 years now, he's also coached basketball teams at Trinity, touching the players' lives, seeing boys turn into men.

But it's even more than that.

He is one of the unsung heroes, one of the people who are the very essence of what sports are supposed to be about, but so rarely are. In the end, the real heroes are not the men who get paid exorbitant salaries to play childhood games. They are the Emil Johns of the world, the selfless people who devote their lives so that kids can play out their dreams.

So when you talk about Emil John, you talk about all the innumerable times he's been there for the people in his community, whether to help them, grieve with them, help them move, or just be there. It's the times he's gone to visit people in hospitals, in jails, made court appearances for kids in trouble, made phone calls for them, whatever. It's the so many times over so many years that he went out of his way for others.

For more than a decade now, he has given up a week of his vacation each year, piled several of his players in a van and taken them on an annual trip. They go to Baltimore, Washington, D.C. and Philadelphia, playing basketball games, seeing that the world is bigger than the mean streets that surround Trinity Church. A middle-aged white man and a van full of inner-city black kids. Together for a week. Every year.

He's done all these things without any fanfare, without any tangible reward. No money. No name in the paper. No recognition.

Until Wednesday night, when about 150 people held a surprise testimonial for him at the 1025 Club in Johnston, a public thank-you to the man they call "The Rev." And this wasn't some phony political testimonial where half the people are there because they have to be, the other half because they want something. This one came from the heart.

The idea was the brainstorm of two of Emil's "kids," Brian Love and Marty Jones, two guys in their 20s whose lives have been touched by Emil John. It seems Love and Jones were talking one day in July when Love asked Jones who was the one person he knew who deserved an appreciation night.

"Reverend John," said Jones.

The theme was "You are my Hero," and if at first that strikes you as a little too Pollyannaish in this cynical age, it's a measure of the man that the theme worked. From Central coach Harold Metts, to women who know he's been the glue in their neighborhood; from a father who once played for Emil and now watches his kids do the same, to a woman named Penny Monk, who said Reverend John and his youth programs gave her experiences "other inner-city kids didn't have." They came up to the podium to publicly say what Emil John has meant to their lives.

In the audience were people of all ages, mostly black, many from places like Codding Court and Wiggins' Village, housing projects that all too often are forgotten. They were there to say thank-you to a 61-year-old white man, a visible reminder that love and caring can ultimately transcend race.

Not that Emil John ever set out to work with so many black children.

He grew up on Prairie Avenue in the '40s, the son of Syrian parents who had emigrated from Turkey. Trinity was his church. Much of Emil's childhood centered around it. In the late 40s he went to Brown, where he played basketball on the same team as Joe Paterno and Moe Mahoney. All the time he was working part time in the Providence Journal's sports department.

In the mid '50s he spent three years working as a missionary in Austria, where he became the guardian of 30 Hungarian refugees. He came back to Rhode Island and married his wife Ruth, whom he had met in Austria. Then he went back as a missionary in Algeria for another year. In 1962 he spent a year at Yale Divinity School before returning to work full time in the Journal sports department and to volunteer his time at Trinity.

The neighborhood around the church was changing. It was becoming blacker, poorer, full of the social problems that have become synonymous with life in the inner-city.

But Emil John never changed.

"They've always just been kids to him," his wife Ruth explained. "Nothing else has ever mattered."

" 'The Rev' is color-blind," said Kevin Woods, 29, who first met John 24 years ago.

For the thing to understand is that he's always been more than a basketball coach. Basketball was just part of it, a way to get the kids involved, into the church and off the street. It was a way to get some of his kids into private schools around the state, out of the inner city, where too many futures stop at tomorrow. Missionaries come in many forms.

"It's always been more than the basketball," Woods continued. "He's always made me believe in myself. And he continually gives of himself and never asks for anything in return. That's just the way he is. He does all these things for people and he never expects anything back."

He always has worked nights, on the sports desk, putting out the paper. He has three nights off a week. But from October until April, his kids at Trinity have come first, coaching them in the cramped little gyms around the state, away from crowds, away from recognition. It's always been coaching in its purest form; not about wins and losses, but about preparing his kids for life once the ball doesn't bounce anymore. His wife always has understood that. His five children have understood that.

His wife also understood that Emil wouldn't have wanted Wednesday night's testimonial. It's just not his style. She only consented to go along with it when she realized it was his former players who were organizing it, that it was being used as something to bring the community together. The very thing that her husband - in his own quiet, self-effacing way - has spent much of his life doing.

And when it came time for him to speak, after all the tributes and all the thank-yous, Emil John talked about his former players, these kids he's seen turn into adults. And as he spoke he gave some insight into why he's spent so many years of his life helping kids he never had to help. Kids who, on the surface, seem so different from him.

"I see love in them and it arouses love in me," he said slowly. "That is the reward."

But he really didn't have to say the words.

Everyone knew that already.

A TEAM'S DRIVING FORCE

2005

"I just think that when you see injustice you try to repair it."

—Lisa Raiola

PROVIDENCE — This is a Thanksgiving story.

With a twist.

It's not about football. It's not about turkey. It's not about over the river and through the woods to grandmother's house.

But it is about the essence of Thanksgiving, about giving.

Most of all, it's about a remarkable woman named Lisa Raiola, who never set out to shepherd around an AAU team from inner-city Providence. But shepherd them she does, and that's part of the story, too. A woman who has battled both cancer and a rare infectious disease, a woman who felt so sick some days at Team Providence's practices she would sleep in her car.

And like all good stories it starts by accident, with a chance encounter between Raiola and a man named Curtis Spence, who from the beginning has tried to make Team Providence a different kind of AAU program. Most AAU programs push basketball as if it's some drug on the street. Most AAU programs hold up basketball success as some sort of Holy Grail. Not Team Providence. In fact, it's almost the opposite.

Consider the program's mission statement: The main goal is to increase the classroom skills of inner-city youth. The main strategy is to redirect the intense interest in sports into other avenues that have more possibility for long-term success.

"I don't want kids to blow opportunities I blew," says Spence, who grew up in Harlem. "And I don't want them to end up in the ACI. I want them to have choices and options. I want them to have possibilities."

It was just this kind of vision that interested Raiola when she was looking for an AAU team for her son Austin. So what if he came from a different background? So what if he was white and the other kids were black and Hispanic?

"I became very attached to Curtis' vision," she says.

Not that Raiola ever figured she would be spending her time driving an inner-city AAU team around. Then again, Raiola is difficult to typecast, a Jewish woman from Philadelphia who went to Brown then married into an Italian family that's almost synonymous with sports, what with her father-in-law who was the longtime basketball coach at Mt. Hope High Schol in Bristol, and a brother-in-law who's the football coach. A Jewish woman who's on the board at Catholic La Salle, and has been the driving force in instituting a program where La Salle athletes are now tutoring kids from Team Providence.

But the more she was around Team Providence the more she saw the inequities between their experience, and the one she saw her daughter Stephanie have with her select soccer team. How in soccer there always were parents around, a plethora of resources. How with Team Providence there never were any parents around and one weekend Team Providence played in a tournament in New Hampshire and had to come back home at night because they couldn't afford to stay over.

And even though she's a fundraiser at Brown and teaches a class in biomedical ethics, the more she was around Team Providence the more she liked the kids.

"I just liked having them in the car," she says "These are smart kids. Great kids. But they have no resources. Everything conspires against them. It's like putting seeds on cement."

So she constantly talks about their grades with them. How are you doing in school? What are you trying to be when you grow up? Trying to get them to understand that while it's great to have a basketball dream, you have to have a backup dream too. Trying to get them to understand that education is the passport to a better life, that when you have an education, the world opens up, even if your jump shot doesn't go in.

"She is my angel," says David Allen Suner, large man whom everyone calls Bear. He grew up in the streets of Newport, one of those kids who wasn't supposed to see 18. He knows the minefield that's growing up in the inner-city, knows Team Providence is not so much about basketball as it is about learning how to be a man.

"Curtis has the vision," he says. "He's the backbone. But Lisa lifts my spirits every time I see her.

Sometimes I know she doesn't feel well and I don't think she's going to make it, but she always does."

Like last Saturday. She was at La Salle for the start of the tutorial program she has championed, 10 LaSalle kids paired up with 10 Team Providence kids. They dealt with a lot of things, from stereotypes and misperceptions, to learning how to organize a notebook, how to use a magic marker. Simple things. Things that in a better world adolescents would know.

And what got her there last Saturday when she was recuperating from another surgery, when she didn't feel well? What keeps this woman, who has two children of her own, doing this?

"Life isn't fair," she says. "I tell my own kids that all the time. That's just a fact. And I just think that when you see injustice you try to repair it. Not because it makes you feel good. Because it's the right thing to do. And what these kids have had dealt to them is an injustice. And if we don't try to change it, it's simply not going to change."

And she sees the coaches of Team Providence, guys who grew up the same way these kids did, guys who are committed to them, guys who have come to know that education is the only thing thatls going to significantly change lives, the only thing that's going to stop the treadmill of broken dreams and lives with no futures.

And on this Thanksgiving morning, Lisa Raiola feels privileged to be a part of it.

AMBY SMITH STILL GOING STRONG

2005

"I just love to do this. I liked it from the start, and that's never changed."

—Amby Smith

WEST WARWICK — He wrote his first sports story for the newspaper in 1940.

Think about that for a second.

1940.

Before Pearl Harbor. Before television. Before Elvis and the Beatles. Before Sputnick and civil rights and Vietnam. Before shopping malls and Route 95. Before computers and cell phones and the Internet. Before so much of life we've come to know as life today.

And the most amazing thing?

He's still doing it.

Sixty-five years later.

Amby Smith is 87 now, has survived three heart surgeries, a couple of bouts with cancer and a minor stroke, and he's still doing stories for the Kent County Times. He still comes into the paper three mornings a week, still writes his "Amblin' with Amby" sports column and does the seniors' page, still goes to PC and URI basketball games, still is Amby after all those years.

"I just love to do this," he says. "I liked it from the start, and that's never changed."

Think about that for a second.

In this age where everyone seemingly can't wait to retire and lie on some beach somewhere, Smith keeps at it. Not for the money, certainly. Not for the perks, because he's already had a boatload of them – having a softball field named after him and having been inducted into something like nine halls of fame. He has achieved a kind of local fame no one could have ever envisioned back in 1940. For the unadulterated love of it, this world that long ago became his life.

Then again, if he didn't exist, the Pawtuxet Valley would have had to make him up. He's always been a little larger than life, one of those guys who walks into a room and takes it over, complete with his trademark cigar. In his heyday, he was the guy you got to emcee your event if you didn't want it to been as leaden as the chicken. He used to do more than 100 of them a year, complete with his one-liners, his acerbic wit, and his schtick that he was just the little guy from the Valley so lucky to be invited here to be with all you big-city folks.

That was his public persona.

Just like he used to say he was the "chief exhaust pipe" of his newspaper. Or that his real name was Ambrose Roland Algerious Jean-the-Baptist Edward Snuffy Smith. Or that he was the "Chief Spucky-Do."

So what if no one knew what it meant. All the better.

The "Chief Spucky-Do."

The guy who is as much West Warwick as the silhouettes of the old mills, the guy who had come of age in a gone-forever time when the different mill villages all had their sports teams, back when sports were the glue that held everything together back before the automobile and television changed the world. He was the guy who had seen it all ad remembered it. The guy who wrote it all down, until he became the town's institutional memory, the one who not only knew you, but had known your grandfather, too. The guy who covered your game and spoke at your banquet, year after year.

All 65 of them.

In a sense, he's the last remnant of a different era, back when being a local sports writer was a big deal, the local chronicler. For he didn't make his reputation covering the Red Sox or the World Series, or any of the other things people usually associate with building a career. Most of all, he did it covering the local leagues, the local high schools. Grassroots sports writing. Year after year. One generation morphing into another.

He's also one of the last remnants of a time when there truly was a Rhode Island sports community, and not just a lot of separate duchies all living in their own universes. He was one of the founders of Words Unlimited, the state's sports media organization. He was big in the Providence Gridiron Club, the R.I. Heritage Hall of Fame, and other groups. One of the guys who made things work.

Jim Norman, the former sports information director at URI, recalls the time when Tom Doherty, his predecessor, got sick. And how Smith and Bill Cawley of the Westerly Sun just took over, doing Doherty's job for months and refusing to accept any payment, because that was what you did when a friend was in need.

Smith retired 25 years ago.

They even had a retirement party.

It was at the West Warwick Civic Center; there were roughly 1,500 people there, and that was going to be the end, right? He would continue to do his volunteer work, continue to spend time with his family, but getting up every morning to come in to the paper was over, right?

Wrong.

Soon, he was back.

Because this was his life.

"I don't even know if I'm supposed to work anymore," he says. "I don't even ask the doctor. I just come in."

On this morning, he is sitting in his office on the second floor of the Kent County Times. It all seems right out of The Front Page, the newspaper movie of life in the good old days, back when the floor was scuffed, and you could almost smell the printer's ink. Back before most newsrooms began to look like insurance companies.

But this is Amby's world, as if you took the calendar off the wall and it really would be 1957. Complete with the innumerable pictures that stare down from the walls. Amby with Jackie Robinson. Amby with Ted Williams. Sixty-five years of memories. Sixty-five years, period.

Which is not to be taken for granted, not in a business where people come and go now, a revolving door. Next to him, the longest-running tenure at the Kent County Times now is something like 10 years. The days of being at the same place for a long time now are mostly a thing of the past, as gone as the days when West Warwick was its own island, before the malls and Route 95 and a changing world.

Not that the Kent County Times takes him for granted.

Two months ago, when he reached his 65th anniversary, the paper published a 24-page special section:"65 Years of Ambling with Amby." On the cover was a picture of Smith sitting in his office, surrounded by his memorabilia, a picture of a man at peace with his world. The section was full of stories chronicling his career, full of ads from local businesses and people thanking him for all the years. As if everyone knows they are seeing the end of something they are never going to see again. That Amby smith is an institution, one of those people who is never going to be replaced. And that's when he no longer is here, and something goes out of this paper, this town. Something that's never coming back.

And when will that be?

Who knows.

"I don't intend to quit," says Amby Smith "I'm going to keep doing this until I can't do it anymore."

Sixty-five years and counting.

Courtesy of Providence College

JUST WHEN YOU THINK YOU KNOW ERNIE D

2004

"I can't wait to teach young women how to play basketball."

—Ernie D.

NORTH PROVIDENCE — You think you know everything there is to know about Ernie D?

You say you remember all his magical nights in the Civic Center 30 years ago, back when the Friars owned the winter and Ernie D was civic pride long before rivers got moved and downtown became as sparkly as one of his no-look passes?

You say you remember the pass he threw in the '73 Final Four, the three-quarter court one that split two defenders and was thrown behind his back, what might have been the single best pass in the history of the Final Four?

You say that, even now, so many years later, no one ever lit up the Civic Center like he did? You say that, even now, so many years later, Ernie D was one of a kind, a basketball original? You think you know everything there is to know?

Well, think again.

For this is about Ernie DiGregorio, but it's not about the past, even if he is being honored tonight, his high school jersey being retired in a ceremony before the Cranston East-North Providence game, in recognition of a glittering high school career that ended in the long-ago winter of 1968. One that will now live forever in the high school gym, Ernie D. forever.

Nor is it about his incredible basketball odyssey, one of the greatest sports stories in Rhode Island's history. It's not even about the odds he overcame, the story of how a kid who couldn't dunk and possessed few of the requisite skills we associate with basketball greatness, grew up to be a Rhode Island icon, the kind of story that reads like adolescent fiction.

He is 53 now, a grandfather no less, a celebrity host at Foxwoods, but if you think his basketball dreams are over, you don't know Ernie D.

For the new thing?

How about women's basketball?

"I can't wait to teach young women how to play basketball," he said. "And the same passion I brought to playing I'm going to bring to this."

He remembers his old agent, Larry Fleischer, telling him about 15 years ago that he should get involved in women's basketball, that it was going to be huge. At the time, DiGregorio was looking for a second act, something he could find to bring the same passion to that he had once brought to playing. He tried refereeing for a while. He spent two years coaching the North Providence High School boys team. He coached a team in the Boston Shootout for two years.

Then he began working as a celebrity host at Foxwoods.

That was seven years ago, the first time he became aware of the phenomenon that was UConn women's basketball in Connecticut.

"I was shocked," he said. "People love women's basketball there. Absolutely loved it."

So he began going to games.

He took some of the kids from the Mashantucket Pequots Tribe with him. He took them to other women's games. About four years ago, he started going to some practices of the PC women's team.

And somewhere along the way DiGregorio decided he would love to coach women's basketball. Once he did, he began attacking it with the same commitment he once brought to making himself a player.

He recently went to the University of Texas, spent a few days there as a guest of the women's program, watching practice, seeing how that program is run. For the past two years, he's gone to PC women's games. More important, he just became the coach of the BABC women's team, the Boston AAU program, run by the Celtics' Leo Papile, that's been one of the top male AAU programs in the country for the past 25 years.

The other day, DeGregorio had just come back from watching a girls' tournament in Boston, evaluating players.

"I'm excited," he said. "Girls tend to be more coachable than boys are. They listen more. They don't come in thinking they know everything."

This summer will be the first time BABC will have a women's team, so DiGregorio is in at the beginning, at the grass roots of women's basketball. He says he can't wait to get started, that he's as enthused about this as anything he's done in a long time.

"This will be the way to end my career in basketball," he said. "I'm 53 years old and I'm ready for another challenge. To use my knowledge, and everything I've learned about the game, and give it to others. I can't think of anything better."

And what does he say to the question of whether someone who once was the NBA's rookie of the year, someone who once reached the game's heights, can coach young women?

"I have four daughters," he said with a smile.

Ernie D, the odyssey continues.

FOR MOUNT'S WINSLOW, OUT OF THE DARKNESS CAME THE LIGHT

2008

"... to this day I am still waiting for my mother to come by and pick me up from my sleepover."

—Phil Winslow

WOONSOCKET — He was 5 1/2 years old when his mother dropped him off at his aunt's house in Providence.

She said she would be back to pick him up.

She never did.

So it began for Phil Winslow.

A few days after that, his aunt and uncle told him that he would be living with them now, that things were going to be very different, and that he was simply going to have to accept it, to be strong.

It would be several years before he saw his mother again. By then, he was 8 or 9, and he saw her only fleetingly. By that time, he had become part of his aunt and uncle's family, his two cousins becoming like brother and sister.

"My sister (Phil's mother) was into a very bad scene and I just felt Philip deserved a better life," says Luann Navach. "And in the beginning, when I wasn't sure if I wanted that responsibility, my husband, David, was the one who wanted him, because he had had a tough upbringing himself."

And somewhere along the way, Winslow came to know that his mother was a drug addict, and that his father, who also had a drug problem and whom he didn't really remember, was in jail. And somewhere along the way, he knew that whatever concept he had of mother and father had been irrevocably changed.

That was the overview, anyway, the hits, runs and errors of a young life.

Beneath the surface was the journey.

"I was shy and introverted," he says. "I bottled it all up inside. I always felt I was missing something."

At times, he would sit and talk with his aunt and uncle, tell them that he felt sad all the time, as though deep inside him, someplace where no one could see, there was a big hole.

"I knew it was something that destroyed him," says Luann Navach. "He was always asking the question, 'How come she didn't want me? How come she didn't love me?' "

Eventually, Winslow came to know about his mother's lifestyle. Eventually, he came to know that the father he never knew had done bad things, and he once overheard his aunt and uncle talking about things he knew nothing about, another reminder that there was a part of his life he really knew nothing about. And until fairly recently only a handful of people knew Winslow's story, his secret life beneath the surface.

"I wanted to be the same as everyone else," he says.

But how can you be the same as everyone else when your father's in jail, and your mother abandoned you when you were 5 1/2 years old?

Those were the questions he would ask himself as he lay in bed at night. Those were the questions that would run around in his head, right there with where is my mother and does she ever think of me? Does my father ever think of me? How different would things be if I was living with them? The questions that would haunt his young dreams over and over, the mantra of his childhood.

"So I basically isolated myself from people," he says.

And he knew his aunt and uncle were sacrificing for him, and there were times he felt guilty about that, too.

Then two years ago he started to play lacrosse for Mount St. Charles. And from the beginning, he loved it. Loved being on a team. Loved being a part of something bigger himself. Better yet, he could lose himself in the game. Somehow, some way, playing lacrosse made him forget about everything else.

More importantly, it began to change him.

"He went from a shy kid with a chip on his shoulder into a leader," says Josh Fenton, the Mount lacrosse coach.

Last summer Fenton talked him into going to a lacrosse camp at Brown, thinking that, even though he had only played two years, Winslow had both the speed and skills to one day play lacrosse in college. That camp, coupled with his record as an outstanding student, led to him being recruited by Clark University, where he will be going next year on a scholarship. Without that scholarship, college would have been a financial struggle.

He has just turned 18, and life is very different for Phil Winslow. And it's not just because he has become one of the top lacrosse players in the state and will go off to college in the fall. Nor is it the fact that he now sees his mother once a year or so, as awkward as that can be. In his college application he wrote about being dropped off at his aunt's house when he was 5 1/2, the day that changed everything. Wrote about how his mother had kissed him and said, "Goodbye, Phillip," then passed him along to her sister, this woman he now calls his mother. Wrote about that scene that has haunted him, and the questions about that day that have never gone away, but "with growing maturity I accepted the fact that these questions may never be answered."

He has come to know that his mother didn't leave him that day 13 years ago because she didn't love him. She left him because she had a problem and she wanted him to be safe. He also has come to know that this has made him a better person, even if it wasn't always the easiest of journeys. He wrote about that in his college essay, too, how "today, the devastated 5-year-old is now a mature, employed, devoted young man."

He wrote how working part-time at Fatima Hospital has taught him to be responsible to others. How playing at Mount St. Charles has taught him to come to practice every day prepared and ready to play, for others depend on him. And he wrote about the occasional lingering sadness, too.

"... to this day I am still waiting for my mother to come by and pick me up from my sleepover. I often have dreams about that day. I freeze when I open the door thinking of my mother standing on the porch."

WARRIORS IN MORE WAYS THAN ONE—CENTRAL FALLS

2008

"I've had opportunities to coach in other places, but I love these kids."

—Mo Jackson

CENTRAL FALLS — Sometimes you find great little stories when you're not looking for them, the stories that are at the very heart of sports

So it was Thanksgiving morning.

It was after the annual Central Falls-Tiverton game, which Tiverton won, 31-0, and the Central Falls coach was talking to his team, players who knelt around him in the grass, their red and blue uniforms stained with mud, their faces etched with defeat.

The coach is Mo Jackson and he was telling his Warriors that they had lost to a better team and that there is no shame in that, telling them that it was only a game, telling them that they had given 100 percent and that made them winners in his eyes. Telling them that there are a lot more important things to dwell on than losing a high school football game. Telling them that he was proud of them, that he still loved them, no matter what the final score said.

And when he turned away from them, his eyes were rimmed with tears.

It was the essence of coaching.

Except that it didn't come in the white-hot glare of the NFL. Or for the kind of money that buys vacation homes full of rugs that are soft under your feet. Nor for the kind of celebrity that make people stop you in shopping malls to ask for autographs. Not in the any of the ways we've come to think what coaching is all about. But in trying to make a group of kids feel better after they just lost the biggest game of their lives.

"We're a family," he said a few minutes later.

The fans had gone. Most of the players were leaving. Their season was over, had ended not in cheers and a big win, but by getting beaten badly in their last game. Football is a tough game. And Central Falls is not the easiest place to coach. Not in a city that's all but synonymous with crime and poverty, a city where too many people seem to come and go in some never-ending ethnic stew, this old mill town with three-deckers on narrow streets, this place where too many people always seem to be swimming against the current.

Jackson has three kids on his team who are going to be fathers. He has another who can't come to practice for the first hour or so because he has to go home and take care of his sister. He has some others who have to go to work right after practice. He has kids from a smorgasbord of backgrounds, many of whom make almost daily sacrifices to play high school football.

"Each year brings a different challenge," he said. "Grades. Kids who have to work. Personal problems. It's an ongoing thing."

"But I have kids who don't want to leave the locker room," he said.

Is it any wonder why he's come to care for these kids, these kids who overcome a lot of odds every day just to be on a team in the first place, never mind trying to win games? But Jackson also knows he grew up in an easier era than these kids do today.

"I was fortunate," he said. "I had two parents."

That was back in Warwick in the 1960s, when Jackson was one of just a handful of black kids at Warwick Vets High School, who eventually became the vice president of his class. He also was fortunate that he had people who cared for him, coaches, teachers, people who believed in his potential. One was Tom Shola, head football and wrestling coach at Warwick Vets, and when Jackson began to coach, it was as though he could hear Shola's voice in his head, one that said to never forget where you came from.

And just as Shola had been an unofficial mentor to him, Jackson set out to do the same for the kids he coaches. That's a lesson that got reinforced when Jackson became an assistant coach to Tony Rainone at Central Falls High sometime in the mid-1980s. Rainone was another of those unhailed heroes, one of those guys who coached for the love of it, not for what it ever got him. These were Jackson's role models, and to him it's all about passing these lessons down. About how it's not what you do on the field that counts. It's what you do in life.

Old lessons to a new generation.

"I love coaching and football is the greatest game you can ever play," he said Sunday afternoon. "It teaches kids so many lessons."

It was Sunday afternoon, three days after his season had ended, and in a sense he was still coming down from the emotion of the season. One of the kids who thought he was going to be a father had just found out over the weekend that it had been a false alarm.

"And you thought the game was the most important thing in the world," he had said to the kid.

"No comparison," the kid had said.

"That's what I was trying to tell you after the game," Jackson had said.

So his coaching goes on, even if the season stops. It's shepherding them about their grades. It's giving them rides. It's a lot of things that have nothing to do with blocks and tackles.

"I've had opportunities to coach in other places," Mo Jackson said, "but I love these kids. They always give their all. They're underdogs, and they need a chance."

The kind of chance he tries to give them. In the kind of victory that don't show up on the scoreboard.

BARRINGTON COACH DRIVES TO GUIDE

2008

"... you get really close to some of them. It doesn't start out that way. It just happens."

—Frank Murgo

BARRINGTON — It started nine years ago.

His wife had died, he was in his mid-70s, and there were simply too many days stretching out with nothing to do, his days a blank canvas with not enough color to fill it up.

And maybe it was because he'd been a coach and a teacher all his life, one of those coaches that every small town seemed to have, the guy who coached year after year, as the kids came and went and the years fell off the calendar, and everything changed except him. Maybe it was because he always had kept getting invitations to visit people, and he decided to take them up on it. Maybe it was the realization that if he didn't do it then he would never do it. But Frank Murgo decided to go visit some of his ex-players.

"It was my way to handle grieving," he said.

So every winter he's gotten into his car and gone off on a month-long odyssey. His first stop is usually Silver Spring, Md., where he stays with a guy he coached in North Kingstown in the early '50s. Then it's on to Annapolis, Md., to see another guy he coached in North Kingstown so many years ago, when coaching football and basketball there was his first job.

And from the beginning he loved it.

For he had grown up in Bristol in the middle of the Depression, had come of age in an old-world ethos where you were supposed to go to work in the nearby mills, the places that swallowed up too many young dreams. Sports were the way out for him, and after the Coast Guard, he went to Springfield College and then found his way to North Kingstown. Five years later he was in Barrington.

He's been here ever since.

After Maryland he drives to Savannah, Ga., to see someone else he once coached, then on to Florida. He sees Larry Kershaw, who played quarterback for him in the fall of 1960. He sees Pat Monti, who played for him the early '60s and used to baby-sit Murgo's kids. He sees others, such as Donnie Blount, who played for him in the late '60s. And on the way back he stops in Richmond to see a guy who once played for him in junior high school.

He usually sees about 10 guys a trip, with each trip lasting about a month. His four kids don't like him doing it, worry about him on the highways all by himself. But this is what he's done for nearly a decade now, every year, something he looks forward to, something that keeps him connected to people who once were a big part of his life.

"I treasure it," he said.

And they treasure him, too.

"I wanted to be him," said Mike Raffa, who came of age in the early '60s and went on to become a basketball coach at both Roger Williams and Salve Regina. "He was my role model."

Coaches can have such a powerful influence on kids. In a sense, they are the true sports heroes. Not the superstars and their Monopoly money contracts. Not the celebrities who come and go. Not the glamour coaches, the new princes of sport. But the people who ride the school buses, often in virtual anonymity. The people who coach for little financial reward.

"You coached because you loved it," Murgo once said. "When I first started, I got $200 a sport."

But coaches both guide and shape lives in ways they often don't understand. Not that Murgo set out to be a role model. No one knew what the term meant 40 years ago. It was a simpler American then, a time of poodle skirts and Sadie Hawkins dances, a time when coaches were often the gym teachers, and they moved through the seasons coaching everything, their words unquestioned. At least that's the way it was in the Barrington of my childhood, where Frank Murgo was an institution.

"You try to be fair to all of them and coach them the same way," he said. "But you get really close to some of them. It doesn't start out that way. It just happens."

He says there are now about 20 former players that he's still extremely close to, even those he hasn't coached since 1969, when a medical condition forced him to step away from coaching the Barrington High School football team. But he never left Barrington. He was a physical education teacher through 1986. And he's forever been a presence in this town, running a YMCA sports camp into the mid-'90s. As if old coaches don't fade away; they just keep going to games.

Last Saturday night, he was one of the first people to be inducted in the new Barrington High School Athletic Hall of Fame. And, it was a measure Murgo's enduring influence in Barrington that virtually all of the inductees this year had some link to Murgo, some debt of thanks. Not that anyone was surprised. He had spent his life teaching generations of kids what it meant to work hard. What it meant to be on a team. What it meant to play. All those things that don't change, even though everything else does.

And now every year he gets in his car by himself and drives around the country for a month and reconnects with some of those old players, relationships that still endure after all these years, relationships forged in affection and memory, relationships he still cherishes.

For once a coach, forever a coach.

Even if you have to take your game on the road.

Rev. Robert Morris, courtesy of Providence College.

THIS FRIAR FINDS HEAVEN AT GARDEN

2008

"People didn't have much to cheer about. And then we became Cinderella."

—Rev. Robert Morris

PROVIDENCE — The Providence College Friars will be in New York City this week, the annual pilgrimage to Madison Square Garden and the Big East Tournament.

But once upon a time, going to Madison Square Garden was not a rite of passage. It was more like a gift from a benevolent basketball god.

The Rev. Robert Morris remembers those early days, one of the last few left at PC who does.

"Every kid who lived on campus, except two who were in the infirmary, went to New York," he says. "Kids hung bed sheets out of dorm rooms that said, 'Go Friars.' And in New York, everywhere you went, you saw PC kids. They flooded the bars on Eighth Avenue."

The good-old days.

It was 1959, back when Providence College basketball was as new and fresh as first love and going to the NIT in New York was going to basketball's mecca. Back when the Friars' trip to the NIT seemed to come out of nowhere, like some unexpected gift under the Christmas tree, not only to a small Catholic school but to an entire state as well.

"You've got to remember what Providence was in the late '50s," he says. "It was a grimy mill town that time had forgot, stuck between Boston and New York. People didn't have much to cheer about. And then we became Cinderella."

Father Morris will be 85 next month, and sometimes seems as much Providence College as Harkins Hall. He has been a teacher, chaplain, assistant dean, vice president of development, one of the founders of the school's Martin Luther King scholarship program and, in 1981, was even the acting president for a while. He's now the faculty rep for athletics and still attends the basketball games.

But those are just the titles. He's also the school's institutional memory, someone who first came to PC as a student in 1941, back when the school was very different, back when Aquinas Hall was the only dorm and the Friars played their basketball games in Harkins Hall, the school's signature building. Back when PC cost $125 a semester.

He was from Jersey City, N.J., born into an immigrant family, and when he went away to college, he knew he was leaving the neighborhood forever. He chose PC because his high school had been staffed by Dominican priests, and the college world he entered then was one of jackets and ties, only about 300 kids living on campus, and Vaughn Monroe singing at the junior prom.

Two years later he entered the novitiate to become a priest, spent five years working in a theater in New York run by two Dominican priests, then came back to teach at PC in 1957. He came back to a school that, though bigger than the one he left in the early '40s, was still basically a commuter school, still basically a school no one had ever heard of, at least in basketball terms.

But it had a new gym.

And a new coach in Joe Mullaney.

It's become part of local folklore how one night Notre Dame came to town in February of 1956, and how the Friars upset them with a last-second shot. That was the symbolic beginning. Two years later they were on the cusp for the NIT, didn't make it, but the next year they did.

"Several of us priests would drive down to the Garden for the games, drive back afterwards, and teach a class at 8:30 the next morning," Father Morris says. "It was Heaven on earth."

The Friars beat Manhattan on a Johnny Egan jumper at the buzzer, and afterward the PC students stormed the court in a spontaneous show of unbridled joy. Not like now when it's as much a TV event as anything else. PC then upset St. Louis in two overtimes, before losing in the semifinals to St. John's. The next year they went back to the NIT and lost to Bradley in the finals, then won the tournament the next year. When they came back to Rhode Island, people lined the highway from the Connecticut border into downtown Providence, where 10,000 people jammed into what's now known as Kennedy Plaza.

"Everyone knew who we were," he says. "It was like a movie script."

Those were the days.

And for Father Morris it's more than nostalgia. For he knows it was better then, everything happening for the first time, the little school that no one had ever heard of becoming a basketball name and taking an entire state along for the ride. A piece of this state's sports history that few people even remember now, the memories blurred, lost to time. A story that was never really planned, but just sort of happened, the best kind of stories.

When that era ended, the Friars had been to five straight NIT appearances and had won twice, all this in a time when the NIT had incredible cachet, complete with the glamour of Madison Square Garden. It was a time when they seemed to own the Garden in March, staying at the old Manhattan Hotel on Eighth Avenue, right down the street from the old Garden. More importantly, they had established a tradition that's existed for a half century now.

"People take it for granted now," he says. "They are so used to success, so anything less is unacceptable."

So this week the Friars go to New York and Madison Square Garden. But Father Morris remembers when it was more than just an annual rite of spring, remembers it when it was like a gift from a benevolent basketball god.

"They were the best of times," he says. "The very best of times."

SILVA'S NFL DREAM BECOMES A REALITY

2008

"It's all about winning. And you have to figure that out for yourself."

—Jamie Silva

EAST PROVIDENCE — Once upon a time, in the East Providence of his youth, Jamie Silva used to run out on the field at Pierce Stadium in an oversized football jersey, one of the water boys for his father's high school football team.

Yesterday, Jamie Silva became a member of the NFL's Indianapolis Colts.

Until yesterday, he had been on their practice squad, which essentially meant that he practiced with the team during the week and stood on the sidelines during home games, but did not travel to away games. On the Colts, but with an asterisk - the NFL's version of limbo.

He already has had one of the great all-time football journeys for a Rhode Island kid, even if he never gets to play a down in the NFL. What were the odds when he came out of East Providence High School in 2003 that he would even be on a practice squad of an NFL team?

There were no odds.

Yes, he had been a great high school football player around here, had one of those magical careers that ended with East Providence beating La Salle for the Super Bowl and Silva being named the MVP of the game. Even then, though, there wasn't a lot of college interest, not at the Division I-A level anyway. He was considered a little too small, a little too slow, a little too something to be a big-time running back, and maybe not quite athletic enough to be a big-time defensive back.

As if there was Rhode Island high school good, and then there was big-time good. Two worlds that existed in parallel universes.

Silva got the last scholarship Boston College offered that year, recruited as a defensive back, but even then he was told that he might be able to make a contribution by his junior or senior year. Might. Suffice it to say that he was not seen as a big-time recruit, the kind coaches all but mortgage their mothers for.

Last year, he was an All-American.

So even if he had walked away from football after his last college game, Silva would have been an amazing success story, the kid who proves all the college scouts wrong.

But he didn't walk away. He set out to try to make the NFL. And when did he think he could play on Sunday?

"I knew when I was in college," he said. "I knew from the guys we had at BC who went off to the pros. And the guys I had played against who have made it."

So from the time Boston College ended its season last year, Silva began the journey that brought him to Indianapolis. He played in the East-West All Star Game in Hawaii. He lived in a training center in Orlando. He went to the NFL Combine in Indianapolis, where prospective draftees are evaluated as if they are show cattle. He lived in Lancaster, Pa., and worked out a training center there.

And he didn't get drafted.

The knocks on him were the same negatives that had hovered over him since coming out of East Providence High School, as if nothing had changed, just the level he was trying to get to. He had run a 4.7 forty, in a world where that's considered two/tenths of a second slow. But he overcame the odds of not being drafted and made the cut, a long way from back when he was just a little kid running out on Pierce Field in an oversized football jersey as the water boy for his father's East Providence High School team.

Then, a week before the first game, he got a call that meant bad news. He was being put on the practice squad.

"I was devastated," he said. "I was upset and angry that day."

But he was told that it hadn't been anything he had done wrong, just a numbers thing, the realities of a business. Silva had just found out that the professional game was a long ways from the football of his youth, a long way from East Providence.

"It's definitely a business," he said. "The organization doesn't care about your feelings. And I don't blame them. It's all about winning. And you have to figure that out for yourself."

That was a few days ago, back when he was still on the practice squad, back before the news broke that the Colts' Rob Sanders was out from four to six months with a foot injury. Even before that, Silva always believed that if he could just get on the field, good things would happen. Hadn't they always? Hadn't that always been the thing about Jamie Silva, that he was better than his size and his speed say he should be? That he is a football player, complete with the instincts and heart that come with that, the things that always have made him more successful than he probably should be.

"I know I'm close to getting on the field," he had said then. "It just hasn't happened yet."

And he said that day that he had gotten over the disappointment of being on the practice squad, that he always had had to prove it, and this was just another time. He had said that both his mother and his grandmother told him that he had been in this position before, everyone doubting him, and he had proved them wrong, so go do it again.

So that's what he did.

And yesterday it paid off. He was told around noon that he was being activated off the practice squad, that he was finally on the Indianapolis Colts, who will host Jacksonville today.

"The dream finally comes true," said Jamie Silva.

Yes, it does.

A long way from the East Providence childhood of his youth.

A CELEBRATION OF ADAMS' LIFE AND HIS ROLE IN R.I. HOOPS

2009

"I knew what (coaches) had done for me and I figured I could do the same thing for some other kids."

—JIMMY ADAMS

PROVIDENCE — It started at 4 p.m., and a half-hour later the line at the Bell Funeral Home on Broad Street on Friday afternoon stretched outside to the sidewalk, people huddled under umbrellas as the rain fell from a slate sky.

It was the wake for Jimmy Adams, the longtime coach who died last week at 73, but it really was a celebration of Adams' rich life, and an unofficial reunion of this state's basketball community.

That, and the sense that this is a slice of old Rhode Island that's slipping away, a casualty of time, and the increasing sense that we are more and more becoming a sports suburb of Boston. The inevitable sense that the things that once made us unique no longer matter the way they once did.

But old Rhode Island was there Friday night, from Marvin Barnes and Kevin Stacom, who played for him at Providence College, to longtime CCRI coach Vin Cullen, to former NBA player Tommy Garrick, to many others too numerous to mention. A who's-who of Rhode Island basketball.

There were people who knew Adams back in the 1950s when

he was an All-State quarterback at Hope High School; people who played for him at Central back there a generation ago; others who knew him from his time as Dave Gavitt's assistant in the Providence College glory days of the '70s; still others who knew him from the two decades he was a coach and administrator at Rhode Island College.

That's the resume.

But resumes just give you the facts.

Adams' resume doesn't tell you that he was one of 10 kids whose father died when he was a sophomore in high school. It doesn't say how he used sports to get to URI, where there were only seven blacks in his freshman class. It doesn't say that when he got out he wanted to come back to Providence and coach kids, the way his high school coaches once had coached him, teaching him values that transcended what happened on the field.

"I knew what they had done for me and I figured I could do the same thing for some other kids," he once said.

It doesn't tell you about the lives he touched, the influence he had. It doesn't tell you about the kids he helped turn into men. It doesn't tell you about the people who said that Jimmy Adams changed their lives. It doesn't tell you how he put Central High School basketball on the map, the architect of what arguably was the best run in Rhode Island high school basketball history, a run that was about racial pride and identity as much as it was about state titles, a time when it often seemed as much about sociology as basketball.

It doesn't tell you about the arc of a life.

All that was on display Friday night, and at the service Saturday morning at the Mount Hope Community Baptist Church on Hope Street, just down the street from where he first jumped into this state's sports scene in the mid-'50s, back in a different Rhode Island, a different America.

He became a pioneer, of sorts, even though he never set out

to be one. If he had been one of the first black athletes at URI, he also became the state's first high-profile black coach. Even if Gerry Alaimo, the former Brown coach, once said, "Jimmy Adams gets along with people. He always transcended that black-white stuff, and back there in the early '70s that wasn't always easy to do."

One of the pallbearers Saturday morning was Ken Walker, a longtime referee and educator, who talked about how when Adams first went to Central no one thought kids from the south side of Providence could be successful, not even in basketball, and how in the beginning it hadn't been easy.

"He turned the losing into winning, and the winning became streaks, and the streaks became fame, and suddenly everyone had heard of Central High School," Walker said, one of several people who took the microphone and reminisced about Adams.

The common thread through all of them was how Adams had helped them. Jerry Morgan, another pallbearer, who went on to coach at Hope for decades, told of how Adams befriended him when he first came to Providence. How Adams became his role model, not only for his coaching but for his family life, too.

Marvin Barnes, who first found his basketball dreams under Adams at Central and followed them all the way to the NBA in a well-publicized life that's been a journey through fame and drug addiction, said with his inimitable style, "I not only gave him gray hair, I got him bald."

No doubt.

"But coach Adams saved lots of us," Barnes said.

It's easy to take that for granted. We shouldn't. Coaching kids is still the essence of sports. Coaching them. Teaching them. Sending them on their way into the world. All the things Adams did year after year, as the kids changed, and the decades changed, and the times changed, yet somehow he never did.

"He loved being called a coach," said Don Tencher, the RIC athletic director.

That's what Jimmy Adams was, what he always wanted to do. What came to define his life.

A life that touched so many people. A life that was celebrated Saturday in the same neighborhood he lived in all his life. A life that should be remembered for as long as there is basketball in Rhode Island.

HE NEVER TIRES OF THE GAME

2009

"I just like going to games every once in a while."

— Bill Reynolds

PROVIDENCE — I didn't grow up wanting to be a writer, didn't grow up wanting to one day work for a newspaper.

I grew up wanting to be a basketball player.

That was the dream, and I brought to it all the devotion and dedication of an acolyte on some holy quest. I ran through a nearby cemetery carrying bricks to build up my puny arms. I sent away for a color-coded home fitness course. And on winter nights I carried a flashlight out into the backyard and placed it on a rock so it would shine on the basket in the driveway, while I shot in the dark and played games in my head.

This was all taking place in the Barrington of my childhood, a time now long ago and far away. It was a time of Sadie Hawkins dances and sock hops in the gym, a time when high school basketball was played in packed little gyms, and all I ever wanted to do was play in those little gyms, those places where dreams could come true.

Or so I hoped.

In many ways, all those winter nights on that darkened driveway served me well. They got me a sliver of high school fame. They got me into a college I never would have gotten into without them. They even got me a college career that would have been almost unimaginable back there on those winter nights, when my only goal was to start on my junior high team.

But I paid a price for all that, too.

Obsessions always come with a price tag. I was a senior at Brown when I first realized that, coming back to Providence on a bus after getting blasted by Princeton, then one of the top teams in the country, running my past through my head like some newsreel. What had it all been for? It was 1968, the war in Vietnam was all over the news, the counterculture all over the streets, and I had missed all of it, my life defined by my obsession with a childhood game.

Why didn't I know anything about music or theater, about art? Why hadn't I been a serious student? Why did my life seem to revolve on whether my jump shot went in or not, my past a blur of locker rooms and pre-game pep talks, of taped ankles and bus rides, and seasons that went around and around? Those were the questions I asked myself then, questions with few answers, the awareness that the game had defined me early, narrowed my options, and that I had paid a price for that narrowness.

So I spent much of the next decade trying to move beyond it, different interests, different friends, in search of a different life. I started writing, and the last thing I wanted to do back in those early years, back when I was trying to teach myself the craft, was write about sports. I was done with sports. Basketball was just something I used to love.

Or so I tried to tell myself.

But every October the game would come around again, a seductress that never failed to show up. The leaves would start to turn, the basketball magazines would start to show up in stores, and it was like I was 12 years old again. As the decades changed, everything changed, but in many ways, it was the same old story.

In the beginning I would try to keep it a secret, as if sneaking off to game was some kind of vice. It was nothing serious, I told myself, no longer something that dominated my life. I just liked games. Until my life began to revolve around them: Brown games. Providence College games. URI games. Any game. It really didn't matter. I was addicted to games, to the point that they had become more important than anything else, everything else revolving around them, work, relationships, everything.

"Do you really like sports?" a potential girlfriend once asked me, a perplexed look on her face.

It was the late '70s, and men she dealt with weren't supposed to like sports. Not on the East Side of Providence. Not then.

"Not really," I said. "I just like going to games every once in a while."

Even when I began here at the Journal in 1981, it was not to write sports, but to be a reporter. A couple of years later, though, a sports job opened up. I told one of the top editors that I'd be interested.

"Are you sure?" he asked. For back then - if not now - sports always were regarded as the toy department of a newspaper.

"Yes," I said. "Because the worst game in the world is better than the best town council meeting there ever was."

That was the beginning, and it changed things. The job legitimized going to games, and what was any better than that? But in many of the important ways little has changed since those days as a kid when I all but lived for the basketball season.

I've been thinking of that recently, for once again the leaves are turning, the basketball magazines are in the stores, the dawn of another season. Once again, the season is on my mind, who is going to be good, and who is not, all the questions that now float around in the air like yesterday's leaves. Most of all, I've been thinking of how fortunate I am to be able to make a living going to games, as though even as a kid I was preparing for all this, even if I didn't realize it.

That's one part. But it's not the most important one. For here it is, so many years after I was just a kid shining a light on the basket in my backyard on winter nights, dreaming my dreams, and nothing has changed. Here I am at the start of another basketball season.

I can't wait.

2010-2019

KILTIES ARE WINNERS—REGARDLESS OF THE SCORE

2012

"Basketball is very important to them.
It's their home base. It's their identity."

—Tom Conner

PROVIDENCE - The Mount Pleasant boys basketball team lost by one point to Hope last Sunday afternoon in the state quarterfinals in the Credit Unions of Rhode Island Boys Basketball Championship Tournament West Region playoff game.

But sometimes you win in ways that have nothing to do with the scoreboard.

That's what is so easy to forget.

Life in the inner-city never has been easy, and it is even less so now, as the crumbling economy has created a mélange of drugs, dysfunction and communities that too often seem as if they are under siege. This is the story of America in this new century, and inner cities are full of kids who are victims of this, kids who routinely deal with obstacles that most other kids don't have. And, for many of them, just being on a high school team can be a bit of a sanctuary.

"People have no idea," says Tom Conner, who has been one of the assistant coaches at Mount Pleasant for seven years now, and before that coached both boys and girls at Classical for 11 years. "They have no idea what our kids go through just to be able to play on a team."

Like the fact that more than a third of the 24 kids who played varsity and jayvee basketball for Mount Pleasant this season don't even go to the school, instead going to various charter and satellite schools in the city. Like the fact that these kids always get to practice a little late, traveling from different parts of the city to get there, their lateness always a disruption of sorts.

"Just getting to the building is an accomplishment," Conner says. "So is getting home. Because they come from all over the city. South Side. East Side. Chad Brown. Hartford Projects. Everywhere. We have American blacks. We have Africans. We have Hispanics. We've had Asians. And you know what? They all get along. And that's because of basketball. If the world was like basketball, there wouldn't be any problems.

"Playing here is a major commitment. It's not easy. But we don't have anyone bailing out. They come all the time. Basketball is very important to them. It's their home base. It's their identity," Conner says.

Once upon a time it was Conner's too. He was part of the great La Salle teams in the early 1970s, the one that used to battle the great Central teams, a great era in Rhode Island high school basketball, the white La Salle teams against the black Central teams in an era in which race relations often were tense, like kindling waiting for a match.

It was basketball that ultimately taught him not to see color, basketball as a bond, basketball as a shared language. It was basketball that eventually taught him that, essentially, they were all basketball players - black, white, everybody. It's the lesson he's always trying to teach to the kids who play for him.

"But this is not about me," he says. "I had my time. This is their time. I have no ego in this. I just like coaching kids, trying to make them better. I'm always telling them 'This is for you, not me.' "

The head coach is Charles Holliday, who once played at Mount Pleasant for Jim Ahearn, the former Providence College player who coached the Mount Pleasant Kilties for 39 years. Like Ahearn before him, Holliday is dedicated to making this the best experience his teams can have. He is always trying to create a Mount Pleasant family, the sense they all are a part of something that transcends the numbers on the scoreboard. So this year he took the team to play in Springfield, took them to play in Boston. They played against New London and PC recruit Chris Dunn at PC's Alumni Hall.

The unstated lesson?

There is a big world out there, one that transcends Providence.

The other unstated lesson?

"They're all our kids," Conner says.

And some days are good, and some days are not so good. For the Mount Pleasant coaches take no nonsense. Many of their kids think they're going to the NBA someday, adolescent dreams that have to be channeled into something realistic, whether that's college, a junior college, a job, something positive. So the message from the coaches is as simple and direct as running into a blindside screen: Do the right thing. Stay out of trouble. Do well in school.

"Kids want to know what the rules are," Conner says.

And he knows these kids have daily pressures on them that he never had as an adolescent. Money problems. Family problems. Absent fathers. All of the issues that run through inner cities like some out-of-control fast break. Real life, maybe best exemplified by the fact one of the players already has a child.

"They start out with two strikes against them," says Conner. "They get here by themselves. They go home by themselves. It's not easy, and I see examples of that every day. I have a tremendous amount of respect for them."

Sometimes winning has nothing to do with what the scoreboard says.

BUTTON HOLE TURNS INNER-CITY KIDS INTO GOLF STARS

2011

"I didn't even know golf was a sport.
And I had never seen so much green."

—Juliet Vongphoumy

PROVIDENCE — I didn't come here looking for Juliet Vongphoumy, one of this state's best high school sports stories in the last decade.

That was just the bonus.

Maybe you know the name. You should. She is the kid who burst on the Rhode Island sports scene three years ago when she came out of nowhere to win the state high school golf championship, the first female ever to do so, complete with being interviewed on television, suddenly thrust into the middle of local celebrity's crosshairs.

And making it better, giving it a plot line that even Hollywood wouldn't believe, was that her mother had once lived in a refugee camp in Thailand, this kid who understands that America still is the land of opportunity in ways so many of us have forgotten.

She is the ultimate success story for Button Hole, this little nine-hole, par-3 course off Hartford Avenue in a section of the city where the American Dream ran for cover a long time ago. Golf has taken her all over the country, even spending her junior year at a private school in South Carolina. This fall she will be going to the University of Maryland.

But I hadn't come looking for her on this sun-splashed morning.

I had come to check up on Button Hole, this place that opened a decade ago to try and expose inner-city kids to a game that for many of them might as well exist on the moon. For golf is not an easy sell in the inner city. It's too expensive. The courses are usually too far away. All the obvious reasons that can sometimes make you feel that it's 1954 all over again.

"The kids know who Tiger Woods is," says Dan Gaughan, one of the people who runs Button Hole for the Golf Foundation of Rhode Island, the nonprofit group that opened it in 2001 to help grow the game. "But no one else."

But the biggest problem?

"There are no places for these kids to go to learn the game," he says. "No places to play. And golf is like any other sport. You either get hooked, or you don't."

These are not the easiest times for golf. Many local courses are hurting financially. The LPGA is in trouble. There are few caddies anymore, once one of the spawning grounds for the next generation of both players and fans. Maybe no game is traditionally hurt more by a bad economy.

Still, Button Hole is here, with its lessons and its outreach programs into Providence schools. There are kids who ride bikes here and can play for only a dollar, with clubs and golf balls all donated, kids helped by the constant support of this state's golf community. And maybe most of all, it is here with its constant message that for the game to keep growing more kids have to be exposed to it.

"This is what the United States Golf Association should be doing," Gaughan says. "This is the future of golf."

His words seem to hang suspended in the air.

Then, in a quirky twist of fate, there out the window was Vongphoumy and her 13-year-old sister, Janita.

"When I first came here," Juliet Vongphoumy says, looking out over the course in the morning sunlight, "I didn't even know golf was a sport. And I had never seen so much green."

She lived about 10 minutes away, and she first was brought here by her father when she was just 9 years old. In the beginning he used to make her stay on the putting green, no driving range for her. Gradually, her game grew, step by step, until as a high school freshman at La Salle, she came out of nowhere to win the state high school championship. Her world changed.

Not that it really changed her, even if it changed her life. When she first began to play, she had a bit of a temper. Bad shots bothered her. But she learned to stay composed, to let bad shots go, to keep moving forward, to keep staying in the present tense, golf as metaphor for life.

It's the lessons she now tries to pass down to her younger sister.

Both girls move down to the practice tee, begin hitting pitching wedges to a small practice area that's made up of sand. From a distance they look almost identical, small, thin, almost elfin, with compact swings that send each shot arching lazily to its target. Over and over they do this, each shot as good and precise as the one that came before, Button Hole's first superstar, and her 13-year-old sister who just may be the next one.

There are several other kids on the course, kids who no doubt wouldn't be anywhere near a golf course if not for Button Hole. Kids all chasing their own golf dreams, no matter what they are. Kids being exposed to golf on a beautiful summer morning, kids who probably never would be without Button Hole.

It's already a wonderful legacy.

Juliet Vongphoumy is just the frosting.

ELMWOOD'S FIELD OF DREAMS

2011

"This is where I got my first trophy."

—Harold Metts

PROVIDENCE — The parade began on Niantic Avenue shortly after noon, and turned the corner and began heading to the Elmwood Little League field, into another spring, another season.

There were roughly 800 kids, both boys and girls, and they came carrying both their gloves and their baseball dreams, came in their different-colored uniforms through the cold and the gray on the first day of this new season.

And maybe most of all, they came through both a changing city and a changing country. For Saturday was the beginning of this league's 60th year, and it came on the day after Major League Baseball honored Jackie Robinson for integrating Major League Baseball in 1947, just four years before the Elmwood Little League began.

Somehow it only seemed fitting.

The overwhelming majority of kids were of color, most of them Hispanic, many of them with roots that go back to the Dominican Republic. In many ways they are all Robinson's legacy, a visible reminder that baseball transcends color in ways so many things don't in this society.

It also is a telling comment on how Providence has changed over the past 60 years. You don't need a census. All you need are the rosters of the Elmwood Little League for the past 60 years.

"When it first started, most of the kids were Irish and Italian," said Dave Talan, who grew up in what's called the Reservoir Triangle and now is in his 37th year of being involved in the league. "Then it became mostly black, and now it's overwhelmingly Hispanic."

Just like the South Providence neighborhood it's always served.

Little League had started in Williamsport, Pa., in1939, and when it started in the Elmwood section of Providence in 1951, there were just four teams, open to boys from 9 to 12. One of them was Bill Langlois, one of the league's alumni who were part of the celebration, and who went on to play for a state championship Hope basketball team in 1959.

"I played for a team called Lovett Beef," he said, "and we played on the gas company field on Allen's Avenue."

He was standing in the complex that includes three fields, talking with several others who once had grown up in the league. One was Junior Butler, who played for four years in the 1950s before going on to fame as a high school athlete in East Providence, then eventually playing minor league baseball, one of three Elmwood Little League alumni to do so.

"Didn't we win the championship in '58?" he asked.

"No, that was '57," a voice answered.

And in that moment they both could have been 12 years old again, back before all the years and all the world's history in the past half-century.

Another guy standing there was Harold Metts, a state rep who coached Central High School basketball for years.

"This is where I got my first trophy," he said. "I still got it."

For that's the other thing about Little League, the thing that all 800 kids who marched into the field are nowhere near old enough to understand. Not only is Little League where the sports dream invariably starts, everyone remembers Little League, even the ones who tell you they don't. The league has an impressive alumni list, from new Friar basketball coach Ed Cooley to NFL football player

Deon Anderson, and from Cranston mayor Allan Fung to Bay View girls' basketball coach Doug Haynes. Talan remembers driving current NFL football player Will Blackmon around.

Then again, Talan has been here for nearly 40 years now, the league's unofficial historian, one of those unsung people who try to make communities work.

And there were some former players who came back for the ceremony, to see people they hadn't seen in decades, to let the memories run around the field, to remember when they were just kids and the neighborhood was different and the country was different and everything was different, except little kids and baseball.

"I had to come back," said Bruce Vitner, who now publishes a golf magazine. "Nostalgia. It's a good thing."

On the field, the kids were crowded in as bagpipes played. They ranged in age from 9 to 16 and represented 45 teams, the excitement on their faces. Eight hundred kids all beginning another season of baseball and dreams, in this league that's been here since Truman was in the White House, and no one had ever heard of Elvis, never mind the Beatles. This league that's still here, as everything has changed around it, this league full of people who give up their time year after year to help kids, the true heroes of sport.

This league that's still about kids and baseball.

Still timeless after all these years.

HE WALKED THE WALK

2014

"... the only way I could repay my mother was by crossing that stage."

—Antone Gray

PROVIDENCE — Antone Gray came into The Providence Journal one day recently, but that doesn't make him unique.

He came with his mother and his grandmother.

"It's their story, too," he said.

Yes, it is.

It's also a Rhode Island story, especially now as innumerable poor kids flood into the public schools, all these kids who too often face so many overwhelming odds right from the beginning. Gray once was one of them, growing up in the Manton projects with his father in jail, and so many of society's ills right there for him to see, a daily smorgasbord.

"You see drugs all over," he said. "You see prostitution. You see crackheads. You see a ton of poverty. You see just about everything."

Then one day a former New England college football star and Patriot draft pick named Paul Lewis came into the Joslin Street Recreation Center to speak to the kids. Lewis had started a program in Boston to try to help at-risk kids. And by some strange twist of fate, Lewis took an interest in Gray.

"That meant everything," his mother said.

It also was the beginning of Gray's long journey, although no one knew it at the time. In retrospect, he's come to realize that he probably was a little more focused than most of the other kids in the projects. He couldn't go out and play if he hadn't done his homework. He had rules he had to abide by. In short, he had more structure than many of his friends. Then, when he was 9 years old, he got the chance to go to Moses Brown, the privileged East Side private school that dates back to 1784, a school that is halfway across the city from the Manton projects and halfway to the moon away in lifestyle.

"I had no idea," Gray says. "I was just into sports then."

But his mother knew. His grandmother knew. So he became one of eight black kids in the eighth grade at Moses Brown, getting on an early-morning bus and traveling across the city to a new world that came complete with culture shock.

"When I heard I had to go Moses Brown, I was crying," he said. "I had an Afro then. I heard the 'N' word. I saw things I had never seen before. It was a tough time."

In the ninth grade he left to go to St. Andrew's, the Barrington prep school with a serious basketball program. He was in the same class with Rakim Sanders, who went on to have a great college career at both Boston College and Fairfield, and Joey Accaoui, who had a similar career at Vermont. Gray was at St. Andrew's for two years, but it was never easy. He commuted every day from the Manton projects, as if every day was a trip back and forth between two different worlds.

"I came in with a horrible attitude," he said. "I was loud. I was arrogant. I didn't listen."

But that would start to change.

Mentors can come in many different forms, and there's no question Gray accumulated a lot of them on his basketball journey, which continued at St. Ray's in Pawtucket. From Abdul Abdullah, who went from Providence's bleak streets to the NCAA Tournament with Providence College, to longtime St. Ray's coach Tom Sorrentine, Gray began to listen to people. Gray was an All-State player at St. Ray's in 2007. More important, he had changed. He did homework. He was the class vice president his senior year. He felt comfortable, felt like he belonged. He listened to advice.

"The people were great, and I connected more with different people," he said.

Then he went to Rhode Island College, where he played for Bob Walsh, the former Providence College assistant, who always raved about him. Why not? Hadn't Gray helped lead the Anchormen to four NCAA Tournaments? Isn't he the school's all-time assists leader? Hadn't he come so very far from all those early-morning bus rides from inner-city Providence to Moses Brown, St. Andrew's and St. Ray's? Hadn't he already overcome a lot of odds just by staying in the game?

But one day last month was Antone Gray's finest moment. That was the day he walked across the stage at Rhode Island College's graduation ceremony to get his diploma.

It didn't come easy.

He is 25 now, and it's been a lot of years, a lot of early-morning bus rides.

And maybe the most important part?

"It's breaking a generational curse," said his grandmother, Cheryl Gray, who graduated from URI in 1978. "Antone is the first male who has graduated from college in our family."

For Gray it was almost surreal, as if he couldn't believe he was walking across a stage to get a college degree, as if he were running all the years and all the bus rides through his head as if it were a newsreel. This long journey that began on a bus from the Manton projects to Moses Brown, back when that was such a long, long journey.

"But the only way I could repay my mother was by crossing that stage," said Antone Gray.

A walk that shows how far he'd come.

And his family, too.

A PUSH FOR FLO HARVEY

2014

"He would average 50 points a game..."

BARRINGTON — Paul Harvey sits in a coffee shop with reprints of old newspaper articles on a table. They are stories of a different time, and they are about his grandfather, a man named Flo Harvey, who once was a huge basketball star in New England.

This is about history, basketball, and maybe a little obsession. For Paul Harvey's magnificent obsession is to get his grandfather into the Basketball Hall of Fame. To get him the recognition Paul Harvey believes he deserves, back before the name Flo Harvey became just another name lost in the mists of time, another name that exists only in the memory of family and on musty old reprints of old newspaper stories.

But there's no question Flo Harvey once had a big-time game.

The old reprints tell you that.

Once upon a time he was called "Newport's Mr. Basketball," complete with the press clippings to prove it. He might only have been about 5-foot-8 or so, but he was called New England's pioneer basketball player. He had begun playing as early as 1900. And at something called "Old Timers Night" at the old Rhode Island Auditorium on North Main Street in Providence in the 1950s, he was honored for 50 years of service to the game as both a player and coach.

In a 1955 column in The Providence Journal, Lou Pieri, who owned both the Auditorium and a piece of the Celtics, said he thought that if Harvey had been playing in the NBA in his prime "he would average 50 points a game."

So who was Flo Harvey?

He was born in Newport in 1885, began playing at the old Thames Street YMCA, and right from the beginning he had a gift for the game. At age 40, he began a team called the Newport Five, which barnstormed around New England. When he died in 1980 at the age of 94, his obituary in the Newport Daily News said that the Newport Five once came within a point of defeating the original Celtics in Fall River in 1922.

The point is Flo Harvey was a star in his time, a living piece of New England basketball history. One of the stories said that he was forever traveling around New England in search of games, back when the country was so different, and the game was so different. In the winter of 1911, he played for a team from Attleboro. Another year he played for North Attleboro.

"He would play all over and have to be at work the next morning at the Navy base," Paul Harvey says.

Is it any wonder he was once called the most famous basketball player in New England for the first 25 years of the 20th century? He once said he played in more than 1,000 basketball games, all the while having a full-time job. He was elected to the prestigious Helms Hall of Fame. He was named to one of the pre-1945 all-pro teams. One so-called expert of the era called him New England's greatest pioneer basketball player.

There was even a "Flo Harvey Night" in Newport. It was held in the Rogers High School gym one night in September of 1965. The back of the program said "Newport salutes Mr. Basketball," with a picture of a young Harvey in a basketball uniform with a big "N" on the front. On that night the first sentence of his bio in the program said that he was a candidate for the Hall of Fame.

He was named to the Helms Hall of Fame in the late 1950s, and by that time he had coached at Brown, St. George's school,

Rogers, and the old De La Salle Academy in Newport, all the while working full-time for the Navy. There were even sports cartoons in the old Evening Bulletin by the esteemed Frank Lanning, one titled “some ‘experts’ are dragging their feet.” It went on to say how one basketball writer of the time had Flo Harvey on his all-time pre-World War II team.

So why isn’t he in the Basketball Hall of Fame?

That’s what Paul Harvey is trying to change.

“The problem is there aren’t a lot of stats on him,” Paul Harvey says. “A lot of stuff got lost through the years. And it’s been such a long time that no one remembers anymore. But he was never bitter. That was not him. He was always a gentleman about it. He didn’t want to criticize the game in any way. But I think the facts are there.”

Paul Harvey was an excellent athlete at the old Warren High School in the ‘50s, All-State in football in 1954. He was one of those kids who lived for sports, as if it were in his genes. To this day he is physically active, in great shape. And he remembers his grandfather.

“He would come up from Newport and he would take me and my two brothers to the beach in his convertible,” he said.

On the table in front of us were several reprints of old newspaper stories from some long-ago era. They are little slices of basketball history. But if everything is different, you don’t have to be the reincarnation of Red Auerbach to know that Flo Harvey was a super talent of his era.

“The facts are there,” stresses Paul Harvey, this 79-year-old man who has become his grandfather’s advocate.

They sure seem to be.

URI'S DIMAIO TOUCHED SO MANY

2014

"He genuinely cared about your life,
not just the basketball part."
—Preston Murphy

CRANSTON — The obit said in Monday's paper that he had been the dean emeritus of the Talent Development Program at the University of Rhode Island. It said that once upon a time he had been the training director at the ACI, helping inmates get their GED.

It also said he founded the first halfway house for felons in Rhode Island. It said that once he had been the first basketball coach at the Zuccolo Recreation Center and over the years had won numerous awards and recognitions for his civic work.

But obits just tell you the facts of someone's life. They don't tell you about someone's heart.

And very few people around here ever had any bigger heart than Leo DiMaio.

His baby was the Talent Development Program at URI, a program born out of the death of Martin Luther King in the late 1960s and the social unrest that sent shock waves through society at the time. It's a program that's helped innumerable minority kids through the years get a college degree and change their family's history. If nothing else, it immortalizes DiMaio's time at URI.

That is his enduring legacy, and it's a significant one.

His surrogate kids were the URI basketball team. And the message he gave all of them, from Tyson Wheeler to current URI assistant Preston Murphy, and from Carleton Owens to Antonio

Reynolds-Dean, was the same one he once received from his father, a man who had to leave school early and go to work.

The message?

Work works.

DiMaio had grown up on Federal Hill, came of age in the grim realities of the Depression. He went to La Salle, then on to PC. Eventually he got a master's degree from URI. So he knew how important education was, knew it was the passport to a better life. He also had come to know that education empowers people. That was the message he always was spreading, a teacher in the best sense of the word. And that's what had gotten him to Talent Development in the first place, this unwavering belief that education was the key to everything.

But he never set out to mentor athletes, as much as he always loved sports. That happened by accident. Seems there was a player named Jiggy Williamson in the '70s who wanted some academic help. He knew about Talent Development from his girlfriend, but since he was from Connecticut he wasn't eligible. No matter. DiMaio volunteered to help him. That was the start.

Soon he was helping many of the basketball players. Counseling them. Supporting them. To the point that former Ram coach Al Skinner once called him "the conscience of the program." You almost couldn't be around URI basketball in the '80s and '90s without knowing about Leo DiMaio. There is a great story about the time he walked into a URI practice, back when Tom Penders was the coach, and yelled "Stop the practice!"

"What's the problem, Mr. D?" Penders said.

"This man owes me a paper," DiMaio said, pointing at star guard Carlton Owens.

Owens left practice to go finish the paper.

For DiMaio always had known how fragile sports are, how they can be in front of your face one minute, gone the next. Once upon a time he had sports dreams of his own, spending a baseball summer in the Cleveland Indians' organization until the end of the year when he was told he couldn't hit and that was that, the dream right there in his suitcase on the ride home. That always was his bottom-line message: sports are great, but education will be there when the cheers are long gone. That, and he didn't want to hear kids say they couldn't do it, didn't want to hear excuses.

"If you didn't get up in the morning he would come and bang on your door," said Mike McPhillips, who had been in Talent Development in the early '80s. "There was no fooling around."

He was standing in line Monday afternoon at Nardolillo's Funeral Home on Park Avenue, and in many ways, it was a slice of old Rhode Island. From people who had known DiMaio in the struggle for civil rights in Rhode Island, to others who had known him at URI, to still others who had known him through URI basketball. All testament to a full life well lived.

And the theme that ran through the room was that, in many ways, DiMaio had been one of a kind, someone blessed with the gift to be able to relate to people, regardless of race, regardless of age, regardless of anything. That was no insignificant thing 40 years ago, back when URI was trying to be become more inclusive in a turbulent time in this country's history.

"His great gift was helping people," Preston Murphy, the former Ram player who is now a URI assistant coach, had said earlier in the day. "He had a great ability to relate to us. He genuinely cared about your life, not just the basketball part. He was an incredible man, and he touched a lot of lives."

Could anyone have a better epitaph?

A teacher, a coach, anyone?

HE'S STILL GOT GAME

2015

CRANSTON — Is this the way it ends?

Does my long basketball career, that once so defined my life, end here in this little, windowless gym?

Does this game, that I once chased for so many years, end here watching a ragtag pickup game, one I've played for a couple of decades now, as countless players have come and gone?

Does this game that once gave me a sliver of high school fame and got me into a college I never would have gotten into without it, this game that has been the cornerstone of my working life, end here?

Because I know it's time to say goodbye, to make my own peace with it. The calendar tells me that. My body tells me that. Most of all, life's often cruel realities tell me that.

A year ago, I was in the hospital for a couple of days for something minor, and when I came out I went to the South County Y just like I always did and got on the treadmill where my normal workout was to run for 30 minutes. Only to quickly discover that walking for 10 minutes totally wiped me out. Big surprise. I had gotten out college in 1968. You do the math.

Playing basketball?

Out of the question.

Even by the end of the summer, a couple of months removed from the hospital, my energy coming back, I didn't feel I could play basketball. A couple of times I tried to shoot around by myself, and the ball seemed too heavy and the basket seemed too far away, and it all seemed rather pointless.

Is this the way it ends? Yeah, I told myself. This is the way it ends.

No retirement ceremonies. No trumpets blaring. Sports are a little bit like life: No one gets out alive. I made my own peace with it. Or so I thought.

The game had been a lover that had never broken my heart, something that had taken me so very far from those cold winter nights of my childhood when I used to put a flashlight on a rock and shine it on the basket, and play fantasy games in my head, ones that always ended with me hitting the big shot that won the big game. It had gotten me to Brown. It had gotten me great friends, and two basketball trips to Florida, and ultimately a degree. Most of all, it had expanded my world.

So I certainly had no regrets.

But there's no question I missed it. I missed the culture of pickup basketball. The banter. The competition. The sense that each game was important, even if you knew it really wasn't. Most of all, I missed the people. The other guys. The few women who had played through the years. The handful of kids. You name it. The endless parade of people, and all the little lessons learned, too. Suffice to say, I learned more about race playing pickup basketball than I ever did in any sociology class. I learned more about people than I ever did in any school I ever went to.

I came to learn that the game was the great equalizer, creating bonds that last forever, even if you didn't know you were making them at the time.

That's what was so difficult to walk away from.

A couple of weeks ago I stopped into the little, windowless gym. I knew everyone in the gym, and it was great to see them. Then the game started and an undeniable fact of life hit me right between the eyes like some errant elbow; you're either in the game, or you are out of the game. And I was out of it. So I sat and watched for a while, and then I got up and left. No one said goodbye. Then again, why would they? You're either in the game, or you're not.

And I was not.

This is the way it ends, I told myself, as I drove away.

But on Friday I went back. I still had some old workout stuff in the trunk, stuff tucked in some old gym bag that had been there for a while. Should I try to play? Should I give it one more shot?

So there I was a few minutes later in my first little basketball game in nearly two years. Did I make the big game-winning shot? Did I find the Fountain of Youth hiding out in a small, little, windowless gym off Pontiac Avenue?

Unfortunately, no.

But I did play. I did make a couple of shots. More importantly, I didn't get hurt. So is this the way this long, improbable basketball journey ends?

Probably.

Just not quite yet.

George Patrick Duffy, courtesy of the Pawtucket Library

IT WAS THE SPORTING LIFE FOR GEORGE PATRICK DUFFY

2015

"I have even baby-sat for snakes, lions, chimpanzees, bears and elephants."

—George Patrick Duffy

PROVIDENCE — Maybe the best George Patrick Duffy story was the time he supposedly brought a lion cub into the old Journal newsroom as a promo for the circus. He was the publicist for the old Rhode Island Auditorium then, and as the story goes, the cub got off its leash and reporters started screaming and jumping on top of desks.

Unbelievable?

Nothing about George Patrick Duffy, who died this week at 94, was unbelievable.

He broadcast Rhode Island Reds hockey games for 20 years, driving by himself in too many winters, driving to Buffalo and Cleveland and Hershey, Pa., driving all night, living on candy bars. He was the p.a. announcer for high school football games in Pawtucket on Thanksgiving morning for decades. He coached Little League, American Legion, CYO, Pawtucket Boys Club teams, you name it. Way back there in the early '60s he did URI basketball games on the radio. And along the way he was a broadcaster, a publicist, a writer, you name it, dealing with a young Rocky Marciano, and some of the biggest names in show biz at the time, forever coming through the Auditorium.

He even did the circus.

Literally.

Or as his resumé once said, "I have even baby-sat for snakes, lions, chimpanzees, bears and elephants. My most tense moment? It came while driving on North Main Street with two live snakes looking to move from the back seat to the front, possibly to take over the wheel."

I first met Duffy back in some lost year in the '70s when I did a story on him for the Rhode Islander, the old Sunday magazine of The Providence Journal. I was freelancing then, just starting out, trying to learn the craft, and finding Duffy was like finding the motherlode. The story ended up on the cover of the magazine, and if memory serves, there was Duffy in a makeshift track uniform, holding a javelin, and looking at an old windmill.

Tilting at windmills?

Chasing dreams?

They both fit.

And why not? He grew up in the Pawtucket of the '30s, one of seven kids in the Depression. His father worked for a local gas company. Sports were the glue that seemed to keep everything together back then, teams and leagues, and Duffy got hooked early.

"Every morning I went to Elgasco Field," he once said. "I would sit in the bleachers and wait to get picked. The neighbors thought I was nuts. Then I'd go out and play right field. And that's where it all began."

And begin it did.

Duffy went on to become an excellent three-sport athlete at Pawtucket High School, already helping to coach kids' teams around the city, and graduating in 1940. Then came the war, in which he was on a ship that was torpedoed in the middle of the Mediterranean. He came back to Pawtucket, married his high school sweetheart, began having a family that grew to five kids, and was on the amazing journey that became his life.

Or how many people do you know that were in the room in Manhattan in 1946 when the NBA was formed?

Duffy was.

His obsession with sports grew into a lifelong career. And if that meant driving through a snowstorm to do a hockey game in Hershey, Pa., that's what you did. And if the job meant that you transported snakes down North Main Street, then you did that, too. Suffice it to say it would have taken a great fiction writer to create George Patrick Duffy.

But how was anyone supposed to compete with the reality of Duffy saying back in 1989 that "when I die and I'm laying out in the casket I want them to put my hands to look like I just shot a two-hand set."

I remember doing a column on him one spring afternoon in 2006. I heard he was coaching the St. Ray's junior varsity baseball team. So what if he was in his mid-80s then? So what if there was no way his players could have known what a name he once had been in Rhode Island sports?

So there he was on the field at Cranston West. He had driven the team bus to get there. The winter before he had coached the St. Ray's boys' freshman basketball team.

"I love to coach," he said that day. "On game days I put my uniform on and sit in my apartment and I can't wait to go over to school and pick up my team."

No surprise.

George Patrick Duffy was one of a kind, right to the end.

And in a perfect world he will lie in his casket forever like he just hit a two-hand set.

FOR MAYOR ELORZA, SPORTS WERE KEY TO SUCCESS

2015

"The biggest punishment my parents could give me? They took away sports."

—Jorge Elorza

PROVIDENCE — Who knows where a dream starts?

The thing about dreams is they can start anywhere, even on Cranston Street in the city's West End, where even the dogs wear the look of poverty on a sunny Saturday morning. Even here, about a fly ball away from Route 10, where Jorge Elorza grew up on the second floor of a three-story tenement that looked out over the parking lot of a small jewelry factory.

Yes, he grew up to be the mayor of Providence, this son of Guatemalan immigrants, but this is not about that, not really.

This is about dreams, and where they start.

This is about dreams, and where they can take you, even the son of Guatemalan immigrants.

Elorza didn't grow up dreaming of being the city's first Hispanic mayor. He didn't grow up dreaming about being in this big office in City Hall where all the furniture is dark and well-polished and speaks of permanence. He didn't grow up dreaming about sitting here behind this big desk where behind him, outside the big window, is the Biltmore and Courtyard Marriott hotels. He didn't grow up dreaming of making Rhode Island history, a living symbol of the American Dream.

No, the first dream was that very American of dreams, one that comes all but gift-wrapped in both romance and history, one that's seduced American boys for generations. He wanted to be a baseball player.

"All we did was play sports," he says. "My dad had been a big soccer player in Guatemala, and we always were around sports."

And in the beginning his little field of dreams was the small parking lot of the small jewelry factory next door, a place where it seemed he and his friends were always playing baseball. The street curbs were the diamond, the gritty parking lot the emerald green infield that was in their heads.

He might not have known it at the time but this, too, was part of his Americanization process. What's more American than a bunch of kids playing baseball in a parking lot like some urban Norman Rockwell scene? And wasn't this all about becoming American? Wasn't this the reason his family came here in the first place, even though his parents didn't speak English? Even though they were undocumented?

It wasn't until Elorza was 13 that his parents became American citizens. But by then sports was everything, the language of his childhood.

"It was always about sports," he said. "The biggest punishment my parents could give me? They took away sports."

Sports were not just a passion. They were an obsession. In retrospect, sports were his unofficial passport to this new country, for sports was a place where there were rules and everyone knew what they were. More important, sports were a place where it didn't matter what your parents did, or how much money they made, or even if they were illegal. In so many ways sports were the ultimate meritocracy, America the way it likes to think it is.

Not that Elorza knew anything about that in the Providence of his childhood. He knew only the lessons he was learning from sports, even if he didn't know he was learning them. Lessons about outworking people, even if they were more talented. Lessons about how to be a good teammate. Lessons about how life is not always fair. And maybe the most important lesson of all: You can always get better.

He played baseball at Classical High School his last two years there in the early 1990s, but that's only part of the story, and nowhere near the most important part. That's only the resume stuff. The real story is much more nuanced. He's on record as saying he might have ended up as just another lost soul like so many others, wandering around too many of our inner cities after leaving high school, too many kids with few options and dreams dying by the day. He almost failed out of Classical his first two years.

But, somewhere along the way he had a burst of insight that changed everything. And maybe it was something so simple as all those old inspirational slogans that used to hang on all those locker room walls. Those about how it's not the size of the dog in the fight, but the fight in the dog. All about the ones about how winners never quit, and quitters never win. Whatever the reason, Elorza found a second act. He went to CCRI for two years after Classical, then to URI.

In short, he made himself better, giving himself a future in the process.

After two years on Wall Street he came back to Providence after a childhood friend was murdered, then went to Harvard Law School. Then it was on to teaching at Roger Williams Law School, and being appointed to the Providence Housing Court, which indirectly got him into politics. That's the quickie bio, anyway, and rest assured it's a long way from that apartment on Cranston Street that looked over that little parking lot that once was Elorza's world.

So is it any wonder he thinks sports are so important?

He says he runs every weekend in Roger Williams Park and rides his bike every day. He also says he's committed to making Providence a healthier city during his administration, with more sports programs for kids, more of a commitment to it. He says he's going to go to all the rec centers, the goal being to not only make Providence a healthier city, but to show kids that there are opportunities out there.

But first you have to dream.

The kind of dreams Jorge Elorza's parents once came to this country to find.

The kind of dreams that people have been coming to this country for centuries to find.

The kind of dreams Jorge Elorza once found in the cramped parking lot of a small jewelry company in the West End and turned it into his own little field of dreams, back when the very idea of him one day being the mayor of Providence had to have seemed as far away as the furthest star in the sky.

Courtesy of the Pawtucket Library

MCCOY STADIUM'S LONG, STORIED HISTORY IS COMING TO AN END

2015

"McCoy was ours, as Rhode Island as Rocky Point."

—Reynolds

PAWTUCKET — It always was a throwback, baseball the way it used to be.

The old stadium that was born in the old WPA era.

The natural grass. The small press box that's up behind home plate, like something you'd see in an old black and white baseball movie.

In oh so many ways, McCoy Stadium always was about the

minor leagues, back when they used to be called "the bushes," back when all the glamour was in the majors and everyone knew it. Back before so many of the new minor-league stadiums became mini-versions of the new major-league parks.

In many ways it was a baseball version of a mom-and-pop store in the best sense of the word, just 50 miles from the bright lights of Fenway. Like the bright lights at the end of Daisy's dock in "The Great Gatsby," the ultimate literary symbol of yearning.

In many ways McCoy Stadium always has been symbolic, so close to Fenway, but so very far away.

But it was all about the Red Sox, too, no question about that. That was reinforced by the blown-up photos on the corridors that lead up the back of the grandstand, the ones of the Sox greats who once had come of age in McCoy. In many ways they were our great link to the Red Sox.

And the best part?

McCoy was ours, as Rhode Island as Rocky Point.

It had been a WPA project, opened in 1942, and in many ways, it looked it. Austere. Functional. No frills. With none of the modern-day amenities. But it always was affordable. Throw the kids in the back seat of the car and have a night at the old ballpark. The one with the free parking. The one where you didn't have to take out a small loan to feed everyone. The one where you could get good seats without having to know someone. About as pretentious as an old baseball left out in the rain.

That was always the appeal, the way it always marketed.

Complete with the same guys running the PawSox, the same guys year after year. Ben Mondor. Mike Tamburro. Lou Schwechheimer. Bill Walnless. All people deeply involved in the Rhode Island sports community. There's no overstating this. Yes, the PawSox were deeply aligned with the Red Sox. But they also have been a huge part of Rhode Island.

Maybe that will continue.

Maybe it won't.

Just one of the things no one really seems to know right now.

One of the prevailing theories is that the PawSox — about to be owned by Red Sox president Larry Lucchino among others — will end up on the old Route 95 land now being developed downtown. The same Larry Lucchino who once was instrumental in the building of Camden Yards in Baltimore, one of the showcase new ballparks that was used as economic engine.

But there also have been theories that the revamped PawSox could end up in Patriot Place in Foxboro, or anywhere else the new owners want to put it.

The point is that nothing is etched in stone. Not yet anyhow. Especially on land that's been viewed as essential to the energization of downtown Providence. But those are issues for another time, ones that are more about commerce and economic development than about baseball.

The PawSox have played at McCoy since 1970, back there in the middle of the Vietnam War. Three years later they became the Red Sox' Triple-A franchise, and Mondor, a Rhode Island businessman, bought them in 1977. He gave the PawSox both an identity and success. For the longest time it all worked, the PawSox as a great Rhode Island success story, a great Rhode Island institution, seemingly as much a part of a Rhode Island summer as the beaches and Water Fire.

But the last few years it seemed a bit played out. Mondor had died in 2010. Attendance was down. Maybe it was inevitable. Maybe it was simply a matter of the changing nature of things. Maybe it was simply the fact that McCoy is too old. Whatever the reason, an era is about to end here in Rhode Island. It may take a couple of more seasons, as all this plays itself out. But the news came on Monday morning, as emphatic as an umpire's call. The PawSox are out in Pawtucket.

Bang the drum slowly.

FROM '78 BLIZZARD, A FLURRY OF MEMORIES

2015

PROVIDENCE — It was a Sunday afternoon in February, and it was one of the most memorable days in Providence College's long basketball history. It was the day the Friars upset seventh-ranked North Carolina, but that was far from the story.

The songs from "Saturday Night Fever" were all over the radio, Larry Bird and Magic Johnson were the biggest names in college basketball, and you couldn't walk into a Providence club without seeing every other guy doing a John Travolta imitation.

It was 1978.

I was living on Hope Street then in the Fox Point section of Providence, trying to eke out a living as a freelance writer, and three days a week I played pickup basketball at noontime at Brown University's old Marvel Gym, which was located deep on the city's East Side, across from Brown Stadium. When I came out at about 1:30 p.m. on Monday, the sixth day of the month, it was snowing hard, which was a bit of a surprise, because I hadn't heard any forecast. By the time I pulled into my parking lot a few minutes later, it was with a sense of relief, for already the roads were getting iffy. But the beginning of one of the biggest storms in the state's history, one that would all but paralyze the state for a week? Who knew?

Not me.

By the next day nothing had been plowed, and I already was running out of food. There was a makeshift path down the middle of Hope Street, and it looked like there was an ongoing party on nearby Thayer Street, with some restaurants open and even some people on cross-country skis. Disaster?

It seemed more like a party, as if everyone had one big timeout in their lives.

That weekend Brown was scheduled to play Penn on Saturday night. It was now five days after it had started to snow, but little had changed in Providence. The streets had not been plowed, at least not downtown, and not on the East Side either. The word was Route 95 was still a mess, littered with stranded cars. The word also was that the National Guard was going to bring the Penn team to Marvel Gym. So the game was played after the worst blizzard in anyone's memory, and I walked o Marvel Gym, and then I walked back, on little paths worn down in the snow.

The Friars were scheduled to play North Carolina at the Providence Civic Center downtown the next afternoon. And the game was going to be on national television, complete with Al McGuire, who was just one year removed from winning the national title at Marquette, as the color guy on the national broadcast.

The Tar Heels came in ranked seventh in the country. They were coached by the great Dean Smith, one of the most revered names in the game. Their point guard was Phil Ford, an All-American. The Friars countered with their senior trio of Bruce Campbell, Bob Misevicius, and Billy Eason, surrounded by Dwight Williams, David Frye and Paul Oristaglio.

And, unbelievably, the game was still on. In many ways the state was still paralyzed, six days after the storm, its capitol city still looking like some frozen outpost in the Alaska hinterlands. But North Carolina had somehow gotten permission to land their plane at Green Airport, the first one that had landed since the storm. And people somehow found their way downtown to the Civic Center, and I was one of them. The crowd was announced as

7,000, but it seemed larger than that. For it was loud, festive. What used to be called a happening.

And that's what it was.

There were people that day who had walked to the Civic Center from East Providence. There were people who had walked from the far neighborhoods of the city. There were people who had walked from who knows where. They were there to see a great game, they were there in celebration, and they were there to say they weren't going to be denied, to hell with the snow. And they were there to see what, in retrospect, was one of the great games in the history of a downtown building that has seen so many of them.

It was a game that the Friars won, 61-59, on a Billy Eason baseline jumper, a huge symbolic win at the time. To this day, after all the years and all the games, it's one of the games I most remember. Not the specifics. But everything else, a gift from some benevolent basketball god.

Afterwards, I walked back to the East Side, through the unplowed streets. When I got back to Fox Point, I sat in the parking lot behind my apartment house and started my car to keep the battery going. That's when I heard the roar of trucks, big trucks. There were several of them, all with plows, moving up Hope Street like an armada, moving the snow as if it were cotton candy. Later, the word was they had come from upstate New York. It didn't matter where they came from. At the time it seemed like an even bigger gift from a benevolent god.

The Blizzard of '78 was finally over.

Six days after it started.

VEZELE TAKES ANOTHER STEP IN A LONG JOURNEY

2014

"He was our answered prayer."

—Yasah Vezele

PROVIDENCE — Last February, I met with a 27-year-old woman named Yasah Vezele for a book I am writing on a season I spent following the Hope High School basketball team. Her brother, Ben, was on the team. He was quiet, kind of shy around me, and I was trying to get more insight into both him and his family's incredible journey, one that began in Liberia shortly before Ben Vezele was born.

Yasah Vezele, who had gone to Hope, is now a graduate student at URI, a decade older than Ben.

"We left because of the war and all," she said softly, then paused for a second. "We saw some horrible things."

They spent some time in refugee camps in both Guinea and Ghana, her father having to pay money for protection.

"God had his hand on us," she said.

In December 1995, they arrived in New York, and eventually came to Providence because of a significant Liberian community here, many of whom had also fled the brutal civil war in their homeland. They soon settled in South Providence. Ben was born the next year, the first boy in a family of five girls.

"He was our answered prayer," Yasah Vezele said.

From the beginning, Ben Vezele was a little different from many of his friends. He had a father living in the house, a father who had once gone to the University of Montana. Ben was expected to get good grades. He was expected to be home at a certain time. He was expected to follow the rules.

"I think a lot of the other kids looked up to Ben and his family," said Jim Black, who coached him on an AAU team called Team Providence. "There was a structure there that most of the other kids didn't have."

Vezele went to Roger Williams Middle School, then to Hope because all five of his sisters had gone there. As a kid, he used to go to some of the basketball games with his sisters and had always liked them. He grew up knowing about his family's journey, how they had to flee their home in Liberia, how they had been in refugee camps. He has come to know that so many other Liberian kids in this city have similar stories, kids who have come here in search of a better life, kids who have come here with the American Dream right there with the clothes on their backs.

And, from the beginning, he was taught that education was important, that it was the passport to a better life.

"I started hearing about how I had to go to college when I was about 12," he said. "I didn't know what college was."

He also certainly didn't know about prep schools, those private places with their old buildings and their green lawns, those private schools that whisper money and privilege, those places so far from Hope High School, an old school that was built in 1936 with WPA money and now wears its years like some old dowager that can't hide the time no matter how much makeup she uses.

He had a good year in the winter of 2013 as a junior. He was 6-foot-3 then, thin and left-handed, with an ability to both run and block shots, and with a body that promised to get bigger. Hope got beat in the state semifinals that season, losing to North Kingstown. Last season, the team was not as good, but Vezele was better. He is 6-4 now, and there were times when the potential all but jumped out and grabbed you by the throat. After the season, he was named to The Providence Journal's All-State first team.

But prep school?

"I didn't know what it was," he said.

It was a few weeks ago and we were sitting in a car in the small parking lot behind Hope. He had graduated the night before. But now he was talking about how important basketball was. And it was not about dreams of the NBA that seem to hover over inner-city kids like Oz off in the distance somewhere. But about what it can mean to him, and his family. In the fall, Vezele is going to Wilbraham & Monson Academy, a prep school in Wilbraham, Mass., that has been around since 1804. He was shepherded there by longtime Hope coach Dave Nyblom, who is friendly with the school's coach, Chris Sparks, a one-time assistant at Brown University.

One more step on the journey.

"Basketball is going to get me into college," Vezele said. "That's why basketball is so important. Because it means college."

And it also means something else, something certainly related to college, but more important. He looks outside the window, as if looking for something only he can see, this kid on the morning after his high school graduation, this kid who knows all about his family's tortured history, this family that had to flee its native land and spend time in refugee camps. This family that saw too many things people shouldn't see, this family that believes that "God had his hand on us."

"My father is getting old, and I'm the only male," Ben Vezele said softly, "so I have to one day become the leader of my family."

The answered prayer.

Frank Caprio, courtesy of Providence College

ONE STATE TITLE, A LIFETIME OF LESSONS

2014

"We weren't really teammates. We were brothers."

—Frank Caprio

PROVIDENCE — The picture is in his office, which sits at the start of Federal Hill and stares out over downtown Providence with a view to die for.

It is a picture of the 1954 Central High School team that won the state wrestling championship. Fifteen shirtless kids in white shorts. There are white kids and black kids. The white kids are of Italian, Armenian, French, and Irish heritage. Diversity before anyone knew what the word meant.

Frank Caprio, a municipal court judge whose courtroom is used for the local television show “Caught in Providence,” is the first kid in the back row, a thin boy with dark hair.

He was from Federal Hill back when the Hill was the home of Italian immigrants, not trendy restaurants. Many of the older people spoke Italian. The neighborhood was close-knit, people looking out for each other. No one ever locked their doors. His father, who had come here in 1916 when he was 9 years old, always worked hard. Life was never easy, even though, Caprio says, “We didn’t know we were poor.”

“My father worked like a bull,” he said. “He was a fruit peddler. He worked for a while at the shipyard [in Providence]. He was always working hard. I cry when I think of it.”

One day when Caprio was 12 years old and working on a milk truck with his father, delivering milk in the pre-dawn hours, he announced, “I don’t want to do this forever.”

“Then find something else to do,” his father told him.

By the time Caprio got to Central, he was 112 pounds, and that was on a good day. The coach, who was in his first year, admitted that he didn’t really know a whole lot about wrestling. No matter. The team basically coached itself. And in a certain sense that was part of it, too. No one had any money. No one had any pretensions. They really had no place to practice. Central was a virtual League of Nations back then, and that old black and white picture in Caprio’s office reflects that.

“Everyone was working class,” he said. “We were all in the same boat.”

And there’s no overestimating the importance of sports then. For sports was one of the few arenas where it didn’t matter what your father did, or how much money your family had. It was one of the few places where kids from different backgrounds and different nationalities could be on the same team with the same goals and no one saw it as any big deal.

"We weren't really teammates," he said. "We were brothers."

Caprio picked up that old picture that was taken way back in 1954 when Dwight D. Eisenhower was in the White House and no one had ever heard of Civil Rights, the Kennedys, Vietnam, or any of the other things that would come to define the 20th century. Back when television was new, and the Internet was decades away. Back when the idea that a kid in that picture would grow up to have a child attend Harvard and become the general treasurer of the state of Rhode Island, even if that would seem almost inconceivable at the time.

Three of the 15 kids in that picture went on to college, no insignificant thing, then.

And the lasting significance of that dream season?

"It gave me so much confidence," he said. "It was the sense that if you overcame this you could overcome anything."

Sports was everything. He remembers a pilgrimage to Fenway Park. The car was a 1931 Chevy. His father was driving. And to get to Boston in those days, before Route 95, you had to slowly make your way up Route 1. It was such a different world then, but there was opportunity, too.

"I was the first person in my family to graduate from college," he said. "My cousins didn't go beyond the eighth grade. My father went to the seventh grade."

He remembers the sense of accomplishment they all felt from winning the state championship. The meet was at Brown, and he remembers eating in a dining hall, the first time he ever had been on a college campus, a look at a different world. More important, he remembers that in a symbolic way he had triumphed over the poverty of his background. For he knows his high school wrestling success, born in the crucible of hard work and dedication, always has served him well.

That's why the picture is so important to Caprio. For it serves as a reminder, both of what he was then, and what he became. And the lessons he learned back then, when everyone was young and got along, back when a team that was a little Rhode Island version of the League of Nations became the 1954 state champions.

"That picture is always a reminder," said Frank Caprio, as he stood in front of the windows that looked out over downtown, a constant reminder of how far he's come from the Federal Hill of his childhood, a reminder of the lessons he learned from a team so many years ago.

"It always goes where I go."

Gerry Alaimo coaching, courtesy of Brown University

BRINGING A FRIEND HOME AS PROMISED

2018

"I'm here for the duration.
I promised I'd take him home."
—John O'Neill

PROVIDENCE — It was one day last week, and I was sitting in a local hospice where my old friend Gerry Alaimo lay dying.

Also in the room was John O'Neill, the longtime Providence College swimming coach. He had been there every day for nearly a week, essentially spending both days and nights there.

"I don't want him to be here alone," O'Neill said softly.

He paused for a second, as if looking for something only he could see.

Alaimo was in the bed that dominated the small room with pale walls. He was sleeping, an anguished look on his face, the sound of deep breathing dominating the room. You didn't have to be a doctor to know he was in overtime, time running off the clock.

I got up to go.

"How long are you going to be here?" I asked O'Neill.

"I'll leave when he leaves," he said. "I'm here for the duration. I promised I'd take him home."

Requiem for a friendship.

It's one that began almost by accident. O'Neill was the new swimming coach, Alaimo was an associate athletic director who walked around every day in shorts, sneakers, and a PC sweatshirt, the former Brown basketball coach who had found a second home at Providence College. And almost before you knew it they became friendly, O'Neill having gotten through the gruff, no-pretense attitude Alaimo often carried around as if it were a badge of courage. Alaimo was blunt, he was direct, and excuses were just another word in a dictionary.

"He would challenge you and he didn't want to hear excuses," O'Neill said. "You either worked out, or you didn't. You either did what you were supposed to do, or you didn't."

And O'Neill came to see that most kids responded to that, as in this often touchy-feelly snowflake culture of ours, there was something almost refreshing about Alaimo's elemental view of the world. You either truly wanted to get better, or you didn't. You either truly cared about something, or you didn't. You were either deluding yourself, or you weren't. That was Alaimo's view of the world, as black and white as the Friars uniforms.

"He never minded telling you what you should be doing for yourself physically," O'Neill said with a smile.

Or, once a coach, always a coach.

And maybe it was this simple for O'Neill: Alaimo had created a life on his own terms. This man who somehow had built a world for himself, one he could live in, one without pretense.

"I think I got him pretty quick," he said. "Never take anything personally, for he always was going to challenge you."

Or, once a coach, always a coach, Part Two.

Through the years O'Neill came to realize that he got to see what so many others never got to see, the big heart beneath the big, gruff voice, the big heart that often was protected by velvet ropes. He also saw the innumerable little kindnesses Alaimo did for people through the years, most of which went unnoticed. And most of all he saw the old-world loyalties he had for his old friends, even if they also would come with some growls.

"I'm not a ticket agency," he would all but bark into the phone, when someone asked for tickets to a game.

Vintage Alaimo.

Then he'd find you two tickets.

"I've never met anyone like him, and I don't expect to," O'Neill said. "He was one of a kind. No one was more loyal.'

So when Alaimo went into the hospital, it was almost as if O'Neill went with him. Sometimes his wife, Cindy, went with him, and sometimes he went alone. And then, when Alaimo went to hospice, it was as though O'Neill went, too. He was there for four days, sleeping on the couch.

Alaimo died the day I had visited him, not too long after I had left. O'Neill had been there when he died, just like he said he would. He also was there on Tuesday in Torrington, Conn., where Alaimo was buried in the family plot in the town he grew up in on a beautiful spring morning, helping to take Alaimo home, just like he said he would.

SIERRA MARTINEZ PUNCHES BACK

2019

"I never thought I'd get this far."

— Sierra Martinez

PROVIDENCE — In many ways Sierra Martinez all but lives in a gym.

She first went to the gym in North Providence when she was just 10 years old, and had her first fight when she was 11.

"She had a lot of anger issues," says her father Simon Martinez. "Her mother wasn't in her life, and she had a hard time dealing with that."

So she would go into the gym and start punching one of the big bags, as if the bag had become a symbol of all the things she couldn't control in her young life. The absent mother. The family breakdown. Her new reality. The bag that always seemed to be in front of her, all but mocking her. The bag that was always there, one way or the other.

That was the beginning.

Just a little girl and her demons. A little girl lost in her own private little world, as though if she just punched long enough and hard enough, she could punch those demons right out of her life. That was the plan, anyway. And almost from the beginning, you didn't have to have a Ph.D. in pugilism to realize she had a certain gift for it.

Which started to change everything.

After she had her first fight, it was as though everything started to change, as though she could punch a lot of her troubles away. Or so she thought. That was the beginning for Sierra Martinez, anyway, and there was no way she didn't like it. The attention. The fact she knew she was good at it. The sense that maybe it could take her places she didn't even know existed. Or maybe it was this simple: It gave her an identity, and allowed her to dream.

Is there anything more powerful for an adolescent girl?

For anyone?

She is 15 now, no longer the little girl who grew up inside a boxing ring. She is now Sierra "Super-Fly" Martinez, of Providence, her father is her coach, and her dreams keep getting bigger and bigger.

"When I was 10, I was a little fat girl, and now I just came back from Ireland," she says at her daily training routine at a gym in Pawtucket.

It is said as a statement of fact, but there's no escaping the pride in that sentence. Deservedly so. For now she has her own identity, she has her own goals, she already has punched a lot of problems out of her life, and now she feels as though she's got some control over this big new world, that no matter what challenge life brings her, she can at least punch back. And is there anything better when you're just a kid, and you can actually visualize a future with you in it? Actually see a way to overcome the problems?

Not too many things.

For this is now what's happening for Sierra Martinez, this young woman who essentially grew up without a mother, this young woman who already has come so far, this young woman who already has overcome so many odds, and sports just might be the least of them. For that has been her journey, and so much of it has come over unexplored terrain. The next chapter is training with USA Boxing in Colorado in May, then a trip later in the year to box in Poland.

"I never thought I'd get this far," she says, full of wide-eyed wonder, looking like a high school kid who just got a good role in the school play.

Then, she darts out of her chair, sprints across the room, and begins pounding on a gray full length gray body target, punch after punch, as the sound ricochets across the room.

Punches of joy.

CREDITS

All columns in *Home Court* were republished with permission from USA Today Network via Imagn Images, LLC. Copyright Bill Reynolds.

Photos for *Home Court* were provided by the following:

- Brown University Special Collections
- Pawtucket History Resource Collection at the Pawtucket Public Library
- Providence College Archives and Special Collections
- The Sports Museum, Boston
- Mount St. Charles Academy

Special thanks to the following people who helped me track down photos: Peter Mackie, sports archivist for Brown University Athletics; M. Michelle Chiles, head of Archives and Special Collections, Providence College; Richard Johnson, Curator, The Sports Museum; Lisa H. Lydon, Director of Alumni and Development, Mount St. Charles.

A lifelong Rhode Islander, Bill Reynolds was a sports columnist for the Providence Journal for nearly 40 years. He was also the author of 13 books, among them *Story Days*, *Fall River Dreams*, *Cousy*, and the New York Times bestseller, *Success Is a Choice*, with Rick Pitino. A graduate of Brown University, where he was co-captain and leading scorer on the 1967-68 men's basketball team, his work has been included in *The Best American Sports Writing*. Shortly before his passing in 2023, he was inducted into the U.S. Basketball Writers Association Hall of Fame.

www.ingramcontent.com/pod-product-compliance
Lightning Source LLC
LaVergne TN
LVHW010647110826
845149LV00014B/2980

* 9 7 8 1 9 6 8 5 4 8 4 4 5 *